Topics and Questions in

Textiles

K M Hartley and J M Roe

Teacher's book

Illustrated by Jane Lewington

 Heinemann Educational Books

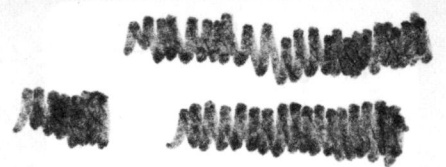

Heinemann Educational Books Ltd
22 Bedford Square, London WC1B 3HH

London   Edinburgh   Melbourne   Auckland
Hong Kong   Singapore   Kuala Lumpur   New
Delhi
Exeter (NH)   Kingston   Port of Spain

British Library Cataloguing in Publication Data

Hartley, Kathleen
  Topics and questions in textiles.
  Teacher's book
  1. Textile industry and fabrics – Problems,
  exercises, etc.
  I. Title   II. Roe, Judith
  677'.0076   TS1465.5

ISBN 0-435-42833-0

Printed in Great Britain by Butler & Tanner Ltd, Frome and London

Contents

Acknowledgements

The authors and publishers wish to thank the following for permission to reproduce trade marks:

British Wool Marketing Board: Fig. 5.1 (iv).
Harris Tweed Association: Fig. 5.1 (i).
Scottish Woollen Publicity Council: Fig. 5.1 (ii).
Welsh Weavers Association: Fig. 5.1 (iii).

The authors and publishers would like to express their appreciation of the organisations that supplied information and read and commented on various sections of the manuscript.

1 Fibres

1 Source of fibres

(a)

Name	Fibre
A cotton boll	cotton
B sheep	wool
C flax plant	linen
D silk cocoon	silk
E spruce tree	viscose rayon
F oil (petroleum)	polyester
G rabbit	rabbit hair – angora
H camel	camel hair
$(\frac{1}{2} \times 8)$	(1×8) 12

(b)

Animal	Vegetable	Mineral
wool	cotton	polyester
silk	linen	
rabbit hair	viscose rayon	
camel hair		$(\frac{1}{2} \times 8)$

4

(c)   A continuous filament is a very long unbroken length of fibre. (1)

Silk, viscose rayon, polyester. (3)   4
                                                  ——
                                                  20

2 Classification

Classification	Source	Fibre	Type
animal	sheep	wool	natural
animal	silk worm	silk	natural
vegetable	flax	linen	natural
vegetable	cotton plant	cotton	natural
vegetable	wood pulp	viscose rayon	man-made
mineral	silica	glass	man-made
mineral	petroleum	Terylene	man-made

(1×20)

20
——
20

3 Cotton and wool

(a) (i) Short or medium length fibres, about 2.5 cm long; 'upland cotton', bulk of world's crop; not so strong as Egyptian cotton. (2)
(ii) Finest quality of all; fine, long fibres, 4–5 cm long; white and lustrous; grown only in the West Indies. (2)
(iii) Harsh, short fibre, about 2 cm long; used in coarser quality fabrics. (2)
(iv) Fine, lustrous, long fibre, about 4 cm long; used for sewing threads. (2)

        8

(b) (i) Worsted fibres only used; fine merino type from Australia. ($1\frac{1}{2}$)
(ii) Very warm and soft; used for knitted and luxury woven fabrics; from hair of cashmere goat from Tibet; very expensive. ($1\frac{1}{2}$)
(iii) Soft, elastic wool from lambs 7–8 months old, expensive. ($1\frac{1}{2}$)
(iv) Fine, soft wool from merino sheep bred mainly in Australia, also in South Africa and South America. ($1\frac{1}{2}$)
(v) Light, coarse and very warm, originally from Shetland sheep bred in the North of Scotland, now mainly New Zealand wool. ($1\frac{1}{2}$)
(vi) Spun from long staple which has been combed; firm, thin and strong because of twisting; used for suitings; very hard wearing. ($1\frac{1}{2}$)
(vii) Long, straight fibre; hair from angora goat; used for lightweight fabrics and knitting yarn; quite expensive. ($1\frac{1}{2}$)
(viii) The finest fibre classified as hair; very soft; pale brown; from the almost extinct vicuna which is a llama-like animal from South America; very expensive. ($1\frac{1}{2}$)

        12
        ——
        20

4 Types of sheep

The *merino* sheep is mainly reared in *Australia* and produces very *fine* wool. There are about *130 million* sheep, producing *25 per cent* of the *world's* wool. Merino sheep grow their *fleeces* quickly, providing *three* clips every *two* years. Each fleece weighs about *4* kg, which is enough for *two* men's suits.

The *New Zealand crossbred* is reared for its *meat* as well as its wool. The wool is not so fine because of the *wetter, cooler* climate, but it is still of *good* quality and much used in the *British* industry.

The blackface sheep produces *coarse* wool which is mainly used for *carpets*.

        (1×20)   20
        ——
        20

5 Breeds of sheep

(a) Fig. 1.5 Swaledale. (1)
    Fig. 1.6 Romney. (1)
    Fig. 1.7 Jacob. (1)
    Fig. 1.8 Southdown. (1)   4
(b) In May or June. (1) Annually. (1)   2
(c) About two minutes. (1)   1
(d) 3–8 kg, depending on the breed. (1)   1
(e) Shoulders. (1)   1
(f) Kemp. (1)   1
(g) Yolk. (1)   1
(h) Scouring. (1)   1
(i) To remove dirt and grease. (2)   2
(j) In a big trough of hot water with soda and detergent. (3)   3
(k) Lanoline. (1)   1
(l) Soap, cosmetics. (2)   2

        ——
        20

6 Herdwick and Jacob sheep

(a) (i) Very hardy; black lambs; wool becomes lighter as sheep grow older. (2)
(ii) Lake District. (1)
(iii) They remain in the area in which they were reared. (1)
(iv) Coarse; kempy; staple 15 cm; shaded colours from sheep of different ages. (4)
(v) Coarse hair which does not take dye. (1)
(vi) Knitted articles; tweeds; carpets. (2)   11

(b) (i) Horned; brown and white patches on fleece; colour lightens with age. (3)
(ii) Brown and white patches; average staple length 8–15 cm; thick, heavy-looking fleece. (3)
(iii) Used for patterned fabrics; used undyed and unbleached (2) by hand weavers (1).

9
—
20

7 The Woolmark and Woolblendmark

(a) A Woolmark. (1)
    B Woolblendmark. (1)   2
(b) E.g. Harris Tweed jacket, wool worsted trousers, West of England tweed coat, Welsh Tapestry bedspread (all conforming to the IWS standards for the Woolmark). (1 × 4)   4
(c) E.g. Wool/polyester flannel skirt, wool/polyester trousers, Donegal tweed skirt, wool and nylon school jumper (All conforming to the IWS standards for the Woolblend mark). (1 × 4)   4
(d) 100 per cent pure new wool. (2)
E.g. dimensional stability, colour fastness to light, colour fastness to water, tensile strength, abrasion resistance, moth proofing, reaction to dry cleaning and washing, pile weight. ($\frac{1}{2}$ × 6)   5
(e) Manufacturers who agree to conform to the standards laid down. (2)   2
(f) International Wool Secretariat. (1)   1
(g) The blend must contain at least 60 per cent pure new wool. (2)   2
—
20

8 Cotton growing areas

(a) (1 × 4).   4
(b) Fig. 1.1 (1 × 15).   15
(c) 100 per cent pure cotton.   1
—
20

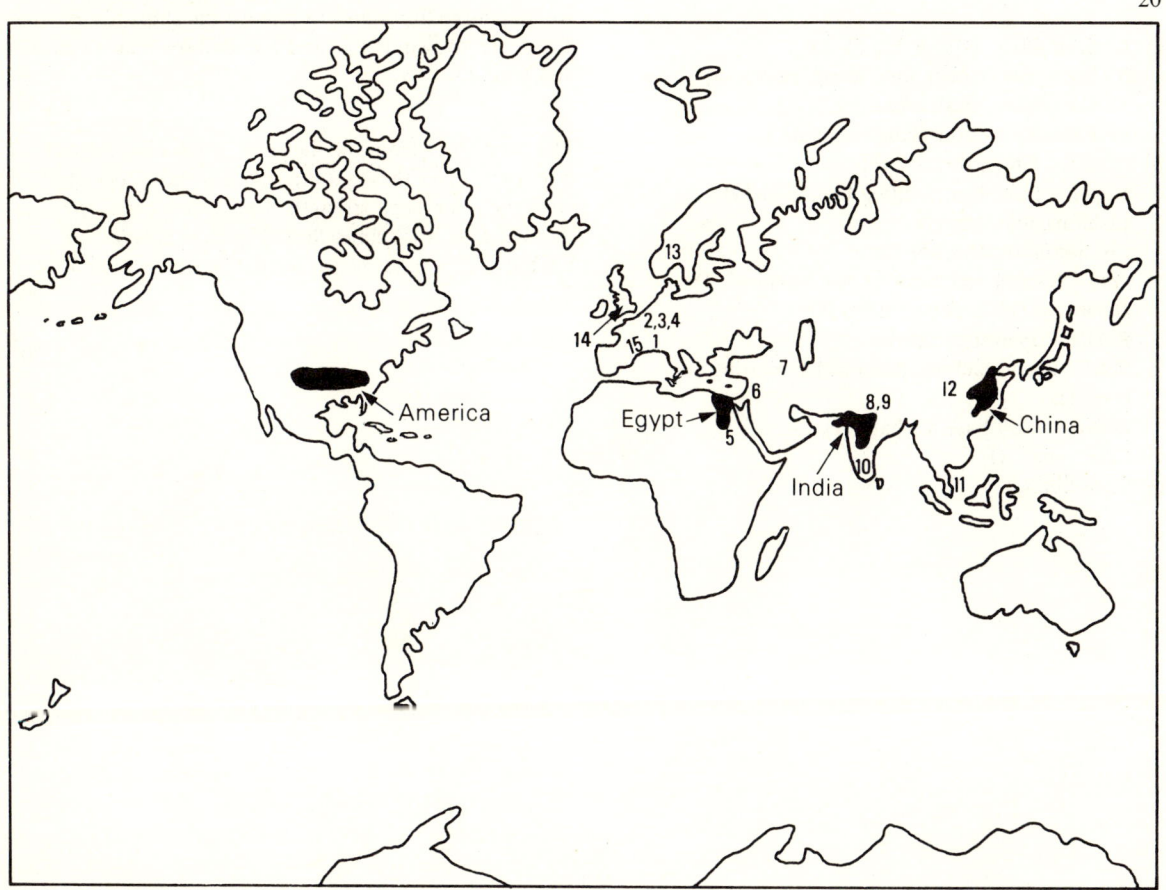

Fig. 1.1 The chief cotton growing areas of the world.

9 The cotton gin

(a) Diagram. (5)
The amount of cotton fed into the gin is controlled by *feed rollers*. The raw cotton is fed on to the *lattice belt*. The cotton is pressed against a *grid* and the *seeds* are removed. A *brush* removes the fibres from the *saw* and passes them to the *condenser* rollers which take the ginned cotton to be *baled*. ($\frac{1}{2} \times 10$)   10

(b) West Indies, America, Egypt, Russia. (4)   4

(c) Where the cotton is grown. (1)   1

(d) It is tightly pressed into bales weighing about 250 kg each and exported to manufacturing countries. (2)   2

(e) Vegetable oil, cattle food, seeds for planting new crop. (3)   3

    ————

    20

10 Natural cellulosic fibres

(a) 1 *Seed fibre* – cotton, kapok. (2)
   2 *Stem fibre* – linen, jute, hemp, ramie. (4)
   3 *Leaf fibre* – sisal, esparto. (2)
   4 *Fruit fibre* – coir (from coconut). (1)   9

(b) *Cotton* – fabric, threads. (1)
Kapok – insulation, stuffing for life-jackets, cushions, toys, etc. (1)
Linen – fabric, threads. (1)
Jute – hessian, macramé, carpet backing. (1)
Hemp – rope, carpet backing. (1)
Ramie – upholstery fabrics. (1)
Sisal – string, sacking, hammocks, matting, rope. (1)
Esparto – stiff base for hats. (1)
Coir – mats. (1)   9

(c) Stem fibres. (2)   2

    ————

    20

11 Preparation of flax

Harvesting
The flax is pulled up by the *root* in the *autumn* and piled into stooks. It is then taken to the mill without breaking the *stems*. (3)

Rippling
The stalks are combed with ripples to remove *seeds* and leaves. The seeds are used for *linseed* oil and *cattle* food. (3)

Retting
The *woody* casing of the stem surrounding the *fibres* has to be rotted away. This can be done in *ponds* or streams or by *chemical* means. (4)

Scutching
The flax is *dried* and is *beaten* by the wooden rollers of the scutching machine to remove the *softened outer* parts, leaving the fibres unbroken. (4)

Hackling
The flax is then combed in a hackling machine to *straighten* the fibres and to remove the short fibres. These are known as *tow* and are used for making *twine* and rope. (3)

Spinning
The long fibres from the hackling process are formed into a *tress* and these go through drawing processes to twist them for extra strength. The yarn is called *grey* at this stage, as it is unbleached. The yarn is *boiled* or treated with a mild bleach so that it can be dyed. (3)

    20

    ————

    20

12 Fibre terms

(a) (i) *Regenerated* – cellulose which has been dissolved and re-solidified in the shape of filaments. (3)
(ii) *Synthetic* – filaments/fibres made from fairly simple substances by chemical processes. (3)
(iii) *Blending* – a process carried out on the carding machine in which two or more staple fibre types are blended; the blended staple can then be spun. (3)
(iv) *Staple* – short lengths of fibre; may be grown this length or filaments may be cut into required lengths before spinning. (3)
(v) *Filament* – a fibre of indefinite length; a filament is extruded through a spinneret. (3)   15
(b) (i) Viscose rayon. (1)
(ii) Nylon, polyester, etc. (1)
(iii) Wool and viscose, wool and cotton, cotton and polyester, etc. (1)
(iv) Wool, cotton. (1)
(v) Nylon, acetate, silk. (1)   5
___
20

13 Terms used in the preparation of fibres

Silk – filament, sericin, reeling, throwing. (4)
Wool – shearing, sorting, scouring, carding. (4)
Linen – retting, rippling, hackling, tress. (4)
Nylon – polymerisation, melt spin, extruded, spinneret. (4)
Viscose – cellulose, xanthation, filtration, wet spinning. (4)   20
___
20

14 Flow charts for acetates and Courtelle

Acetate – wood pulp and cotton linters (1)	*Courtelle* – acryloni- trile (1)
acetylation	polymerisation
ripening	extrusion
precipitation	stretching
drying	washing
spinning solution formed	drying
filtration	stabilising
dry spinning	crimping
continuous filament yarn	cutting
staple fibre (1 × 9)	spinning (1 × 9) 20

___
20

15 Microscopic appearance of fibres (1)

Silk E 4
Cotton A 3
Linen C 2
Orlon G 7
Wool D 5
Polyester F 6
Polyamide J 8
Viscose B 1
Acetate I 9
Mercerised cotton H 10   (2 × 10)   20
___
20

16 Microscopic appearance of fibres (2)

(a) Fig. 1.2 (2 × 6).   12
(b) Fig. 1.3 (2 × 4).   8
                        ——
                        20

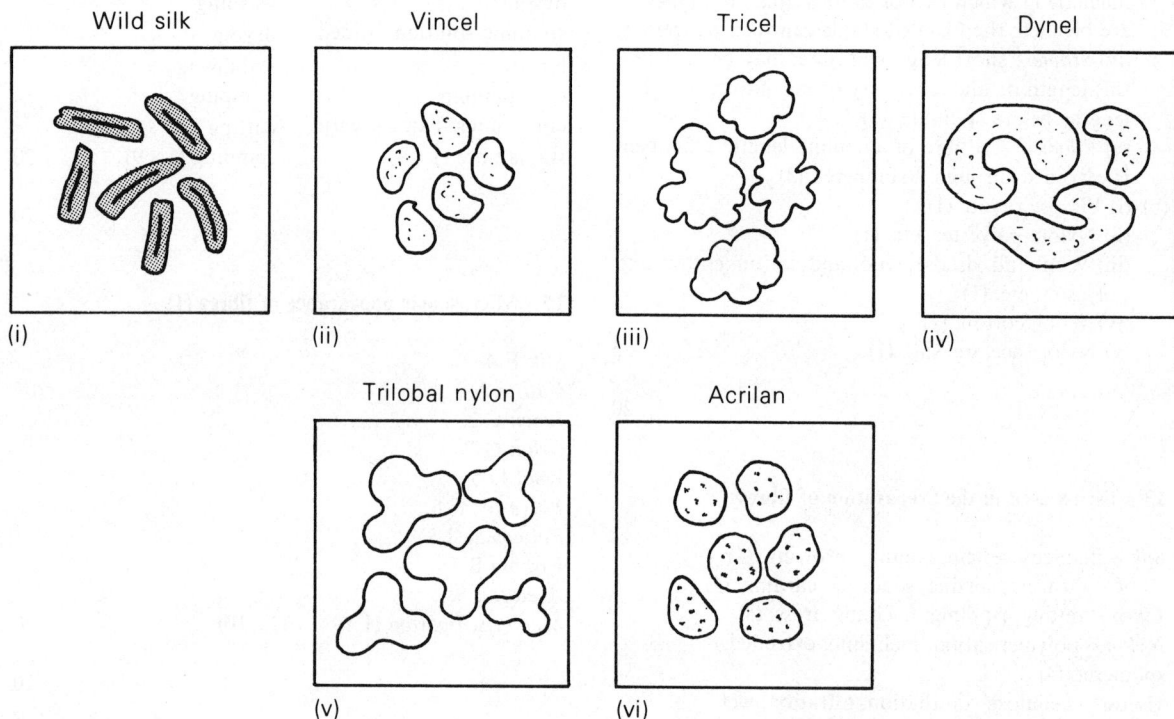

Fig. 1.2

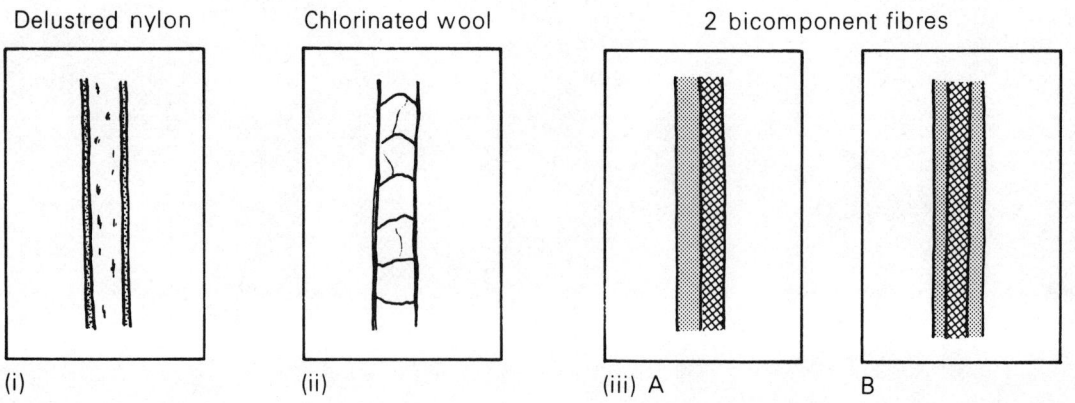

Fig. 1.3

17 Bulking of synthetics

(a) Traps air between fibres so the fabric is warmer; it absorbs moisture more readily. (2)   2

(b) The stuffer box method is used for the production of *Ban-lon*. The yarn is *stuffed* into a *heated* box and this causes the *filaments* to have a *zig-zag* shape which remains on *cooling*.   6

(c) *Air texturing* (1) – yarn passes through a strong current of air causing the filaments to form small loops (1) – Taslan (1). Diagram (Fig. 1.4) (1).
Edge crimp (1) – the filament yarn is pulled over a sharp edge to give it a crimp (1) – Agilon (1). Diagram (Fig. 1.5) (1).
Knit-de-knit (1) – yarn knitted, heat set, then unravelled (1) – Buclon, trilobal nylon (1). Diagram (Fig. 1.6) (1).   12

     ——
     20

Fig. 1.4   Air texturing.

Fig. 1.5 Edge crimp.

Fig. 1.6   Knit-de-knit.

18 Burning tests for fibre identification

(a) Ease of melting or catching fire and appearance during burning (1), smell (odour) (1), ability to burn when removed from the flame (1), appearance of residue (1).   4

(b)

Polyester	black sooty flame; aromatic smell; shrinks from flame; hard black bead.
Wool	spluttering; smell of burning hair; no bead formed; flame does not spread.
Cotton	vigorous burning; smell of burning paper; carries on burning when flame is removed; soft grey ash.
Tricel	burns quickly; smell of vinegar; runs away from flame; leaves hard glassy black bead.

     (4 × 4)

     16
     ——
     20

19 Multiple-choice questions

(a) D (b) A (c) C (d) C (e) D (f) D (g) B (h) B
(i) C (j) B (k) D (l) D (m) D (n) D (o) B (p) D
(q) A (r) A (s) D (t) A.

     1 × 20)   20
     ——
     20

2 Yarns

1 Sewing thread types

Thread type	Fibre content
tacking thread	cotton
Sylko	cotton
machine cotton	cotton
Anchor machine embroidery	cotton
Drima Bold	Polyester
Gütermann Goliath	Polyester
button thread	linen
strong thread	linen
pure silk machine thread	silk
Dewhurst Star	polyester
Drima	polyester
Coats poly/cotton	blend of polyester and cotton
Gütermann M113	polyester
Mölnlycke (grey reel)	polyester
invisible	plastic
coton à broder	cotton
Anchor stranded	cotton
Anchor soft	cotton
Perle	cotton
tapestry wool	wool
crewel wool	wool
mending wool	wool
($\frac{1}{2} \times 20$)	($\frac{1}{2} \times 20$)	20

20

2 Packaging of threads

(a) A – cop, B – cone, C – cocoon, D – reel. (4)   4

(b) A – Dewhurst (1), Sylko ($\frac{1}{2}$).
B – Coats (1), Drima ($\frac{1}{2}$).
C – Gütermann (1), 100 per cent polyester ($\frac{1}{2}$).
D – Dewhurst (1), Star ($\frac{1}{2}$).   6

(c) (i) 'z' twist   1
(ii) *mercerised* – adds lustre; increases tensile strength. (2)
gassed – singed to remove surface hairs. (2)
glacé – polished; extra strength; increases resistance to abrasion; good for stitching leather. (3)   7
(iii) 36, 40, 50; finest is 50. ($\frac{1}{2} \times 4$)   2

20

3 Lurex

(a) Lurex is really a fine sheet of *metal* sandwiched between *two* thin *layers* of *plastic* and then *split* into yarns the required *width*. This is known as a *laminated* yarn. Lurex is often *twisted* with *wool* or Courtelle and made into a *knitting* or weaving *yarn*. This is a *blended* yarn.   12

(b) *Buttonhole gimp* – wrapped yarn; 3 ply; cotton core; rayon, silk or mercerised cotton wrapping. (4)
Shirring elastic – wrapped yarn; single elastic core; double layer of cotton wrapping. (4)   8

20

4 The spinning wheel

(a) 1 treadle, 2 'mother-of-all', 3 spindle, 4 maidens, 5 distaff, 6 distaff holder, 7 flyer, 8 belt, 9 wheel, 10 crank. (1 × 10)   10

(b) The treadle is pushed with the feet and forces the crank to drive the wheel. The belt fits into a groove in the wheel which then drives the spindle by means of a smaller wheel. The spindle rotates very quickly. The flyer helps to spread the yarn evenly on the spindle. (The spindle is held between the maidens, the whole of this section being known as the 'mother-of-all'.) The distaff holds the carded wool ready for spinning.   10

20

5 Carding

Carding produces a *sliver* suitable for most yarn manufacture, but for *high* quality yarns the *short* fibres have to be *removed*. To do this the sliver is *combed*. Cotton and wool can be treated in this way. The short wool fibres are called *noil* and are used for *felt* making and the resulting *long* fibres are used to make *worsted*. Ben *Noble* invented a *combing* machine in 1853 and this method is still used. Only after *drawing* and *drafting* to make the sliver finer is it suitable for *spinning*.

During spinning the yarn is *twisted* and *wound* onto a *bobbin*. Various gadgets are used to ensure that the yarn is wound *evenly* on the bobbin. There are two main methods of spinning – *mule* spinning and *ring* spinning. (1 × 20) 20

—

20

6 Terms used in connection with yarns

(a) Felt. (1) 1
(b) Weft knitting. (1) 1
(c) Two – warp and weft. (3) 3
(d) S and z. (2) 2
(e) Ply. (1) 1
(f) Strength, thickness, smoothness, 'z' twist. (3) 3
(g) (i) Denier. (1)
    (ii) 12. (1) 2
(h) A *distaff* and *spindle* were used in the primitive spinning of yarn when a *spinning wheel* was used. In the year *1768* James *Hargreaves* invented the spinning *jenny* which greatly increased the rate of production. 7

—

20

7 Inventors

(a)
James Hargreaves	spinning jenny	1768
Eli Whitney	cotton gin	1793
John Kay	flying shuttle	1733
Richard Arkwright	water frame	1768
Samuel Compton	spinning mule	1779
Edmund Cartwright	power loom	1787
Joseph Jacquard	pattern loom	1801

(7 + 7) 14

(b) Climate suitable for spinning cotton; streams flowing into the Ribble and Mersey supplied water power for the first mills; plenty of coal available locally; water in Lancashire was particularly suitable for bleaching and the calico printing processes. (2) 2
(c) Steam engine; Watt. (2) 2
(d) Spinning became a factory industry (1) 1
(e) Spinning had been done by women so they came to be known as 'spinsters'. (1) 1

—

20

8 Fancy yarns

(a) (i) C (chenille). ($\frac{1}{2}$)
    (ii) A (printed). ($\frac{1}{2}$)
    (iii) B (slub). ($\frac{1}{2}$) $1\frac{1}{2}$
(b) (i) leno. (1)

Key:—Warp
    Weft
    Warp   (3)

    (ii) To allow for cutting so that yarn may be produced. (2)
    (iii) Chenille. (1) 7
(c) Printed yarn is dark and light in definite predetermined sections. Random dyed yarn shades gradually from one colour to the next. (5) 5
(d) Labelled diagram (Fig. 2.1) ($\frac{1}{2}$ × 3) $1\frac{1}{2}$
(e) Two different colours are spun together at different speeds, alternately to form knops. A yarn of loose twist is then added. (5) 5

—

20

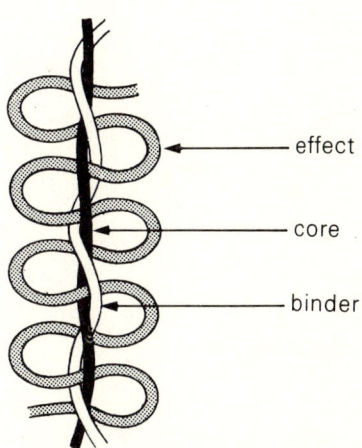

Fig. 2.1   A composite effect yarn.

9 Filament yarns – tex and denier

(a) Yarn made up of several filaments. (1)   1

(b) Strength; hardwearing; more flexible; more elastic. (4)   4

(c) Single; coarse; twistless filament; stretched while hot; usually nylon; stiff; colourless; used in construction of manufactured clothing to save colour matching. (7)   7

(d) Used to describe the coarseness of yarn – the weight in grams of 1000 metres of yarn. (3)   3

(e) Used to describe the fineness of yarn – one denier is the weight in grams of 9,000 metres of yarn. (4)   4

(f) iv. (1)   1

                                    —

                                  20

10 Blending and high bulking

(a) *Economy* – blended yarns are often cheaper, e.g. wool and polyester would be cheaper than all wool.

Improving properties e.g. increasing crease resistance by blending linen and polyester; easier laundering – blending cotton and polyester.

Creating novelty or textural effects – add lurex to any yarn for novelty; add mohair for luxury.

Variety – giving a wider range of yarns. (3×4) 12

(b) Blended yarn (1); two types of acrylic fibre (1); one high and one low shrinkage potential (2); fibres subject to heat during manufacture (1) and shrinkage takes place (1); some fibres longer and become crimped (1); bulk and warmth increased (1).   8

                                    —

                                  20

3 Fabrics

1 Weaving and knitting

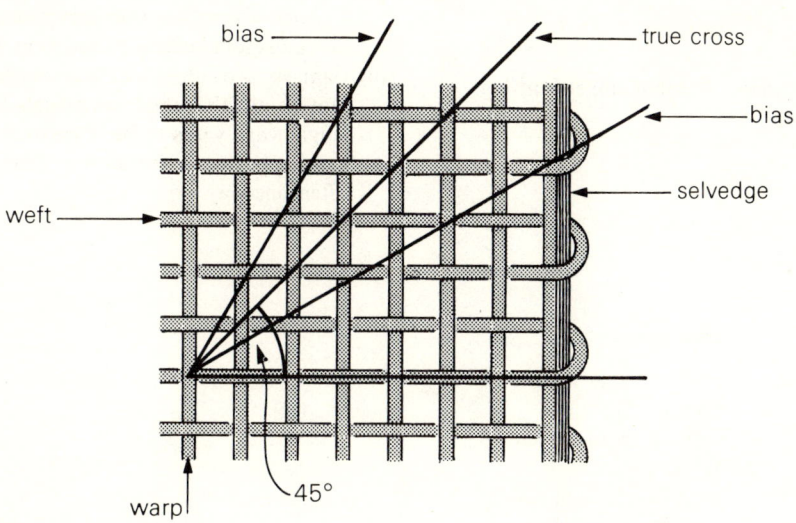

Fig. 3.1   Weaving.

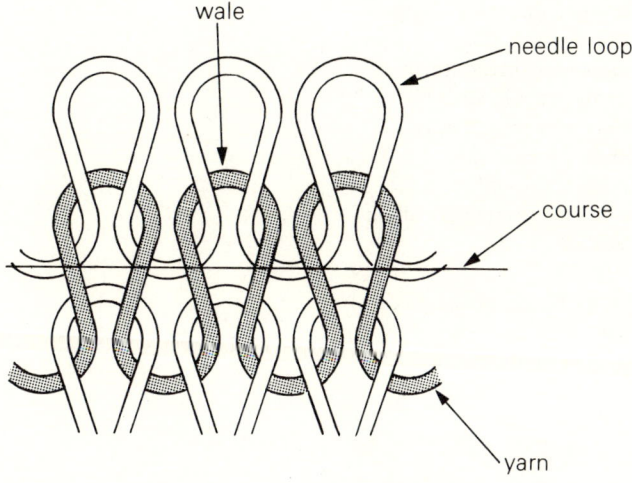

Fig. 3.2   Weft knitting.

2 Tools used for making fabrics

(a)

	Tool	Use
A	crochet hook	crochet
B	tatting shuttle	tatting
C	dolly bobbin	French knitting
D	lace bobbin	lace
E	latch needle	knitting (by machine)
F	shuttle	weaving
G	Tunisian crochet hook	crochet
H	netting needle	knotting and netting
I	pair of knitting needles	knitting

(1×9) $(\frac{1}{2} \times 9)$ $13\frac{1}{2}$

(b) *Hand crafts* – A, B, C, D, G, H, I. $(\frac{1}{2} \times 7)$
    Factory used – E, F. $(\frac{1}{2} \times 2)$ $4\frac{1}{2}$

(c) E.g. macramé, plaiting, braiding, finger knitting.
(1×2) 2
                ——
                20

3 The loom

(a)

	Part	Function
1	warp beam (1)	roller to hold warp threads (1)
2	cloth beam (1)	roller to hold woven fabric (1)
3	shed (1)	opening through which shuttle passes when warp threads are raised (2)
4	heddles (1)	wires with a central hole through which one warp thread passes (2)
5	shuttle (1)	holds weft thread, thrown across warp in shed (2)
6	reed (1)	beats weft thread into fabric position (2)
7	weft yarn (1)	forms width of fabric sometimes known as filling yarn (2)

                19

(b) The selvedge is formed at each side of the piece of fabric as the weft yarn turns back over the end warp thread. (1)

                1
                ——
                20

4 Weaves (1)

(a)

A Plain weave (1) – the weft threads pass over and under one warp thread alternatively. (3)

B Hopsack or basket weave (1) – two rows of weft threads pass alternately under and over two warp threads. (3)

C Twill weave (1) – weft yarn goes over three warp threads and under one, moving along one warp thread on each row – gives a diagonal effect, 'z' direction. (3)

D Twill weave (1) – weft yarn passes over two warp threads and under two, moving one warp thread on each row – gives a diagonal effect, 'z' direction. (3)   16

(b) damask, brocade. (1) Colour and pattern are woven into the fabric; complicated machine enables single warp yarns to be lifted so curves and shapes can be produced; fabrics fray easily; designs are often one-way. (3)   4
                ——
                20

5 Weaves (2)

(a) Diagram of herringbone weave (Fig. 3.3) (2);
   diagram of satin weave (Fig. 3.4) (2).   4

(b) *Satin weave* – warp threads are the floats. $(1\frac{1}{2})$
   Sateen weave – weft thread passes over five or
   more warp yarns. $(1\frac{1}{2})$ 3

(c) A All over pile (1); velveteen (1).
   B Pile in rows down length of fabric, longer
   pile (2); corduroy (1).   5

(d) Needlecord, velvet, terry towelling, velour, camel
   cloth, candlewick. (1 mark for each name and 3
   marks for each description.)   8
                                                            ___
                                                             20

Fig. 3.3   Herringbone weave.

Fig. 3.4   Satin weave.

6 Knitted constructions

(a) *Warp knitting*
   One thread is supplied to each *needle* and produces
   a row of *loops* down the fabric. The *threads* are
   moved from one needle to another on successive
   courses. (5)

   Warp knitted locknit
   This is the most widely used method of warp
   knitting. There are *two* threads to each needle. The
   fabric will not *ladder* and it has a *smooth* surface. (3)

   Warp knitted net
   This fabric has *diamond* shaped openings. A *single*
   thread is used. It is often used in the manufacture
   of *curtains*. (3)   11

(b) (i) A First loop in hook.(1)
      B Needle moves forward and first loop opens
      latch and slips over it, new yarn laid in hook. (3)
      C Needle moves back and latch is closed as
      first loop slips over the hook. (3)
      D The new thread is now in the hook. (1)
   (ii) Crochet. (1)   9
                                                            ___
                                                             20

7 Blended fabrics – Viyella and Clydella

(a) Viyella is a blended fabric which carries the
   Woolblendmark. The fibre content is *55 per cent*
   wool and *45 per cent* cotton. It is always made in
   a *2 × 2 twill* weave. The cloth can be *colour woven,
   printed* or dyed.
      Clydella is also a *blended* fabric made from 80
   per cent *cotton* and 20 per cent *wool*.   10

(b) The blend does not contain sufficient wool
   to qualify for the Woolblendmark. (1)   1

(c) Plain weave; 20 per cent wool and 80 per cent
   cotton; lightweight; soft to handle; good drape;
   washable; printed or plain. (6)   6

(d) *Viyella* – child's dress. (1)
   Clydella – school shirt. (1)
   Viyella lawn – evening blouse. (1)   3
                                                            ___
                                                             20

8 Blended fabrics – Vilene

(a) Polyester, nylon, viscose, acrylic, cotton, acetate. (4) 4

(b) Vilene is a non-woven fabric. The carded *web* is *bonded* by adhesives and produces a fabric which is widely used for *interfacings*. Many different weights are produced in both *iron-on* and *sew-in* varieties. Sew-in varieties are machined on the *fitting* line or invisibly sewn with *catch* stitch on *folded* edges. When using iron-on varieties and in order to obtain a good bond to the fabric a *damp muslin* cloth and a *hot* iron should be used. The fabric must then be left to *cool* before handling to give the *adhesive* time to *set*. 14

(c) An adhesive web – made from granules which are melted and converted into adhesive fibres (1); used to fix hems, facings, etc. without sewing (1). 2
                                                                                        ——
                                                                                        20

9 Plain weave

(a) Graph paper; small squares; thicker lines; used for diagrams and patterns; squares filled in where warp passes over weft. (4) 4

(b) Fig. 3.11.1 Photograph. (1)
Fig. 3.11.2
A Point paper. (1)
B Sections through warp and weft. (1)
C Weave diagram. (1) 4

(c) (i) A counting glass. (1)
1 In the top section is a lens. (1)
2, 4 These are hinges which enable it to fold flat. (2)
3 This is the side support. (1)
5 This is the base plate in which is a cut out shape of known area. (2)
The counting glass is usually made of metal although some plastic ones are now available. (1)
(ii) It is placed on top of a piece of woven fabric which is to be analysed. On looking through the lens the threads can be counted and the number in a given area found. (4) 12
                                                                                        ——
                                                                                        20

10 Woven fabrics

Fabric	Fibre	Classification
huckaback	linen (flax)	vegetable – cellulose
flannelette	cotton	vegetable – cellulose
flannel	wool	animal – protein
tussah	silk	animal – protein
duck	linen (flax)	vegetable – cellulose
ninon	silk	animal – protein
sateen	cotton	vegetable – cellulose
serge	wool	animal – protein
taffeta	silk	animal – protein
barathea	wool	animal – protein
	(1×10)	(1×10) 20

——
20

11 Fabric descriptions

Examples only:
gingham 6, 12, 13, 14, 16. Any four (4).
organdie 1, 6, 10, 14, 16. Any four (4).
wool tweed 2, 3, 6, 9, 14, 15, 16. Any four (4).
corduroy 2, 5, 11, 12, 13. Any four (4).
denim 2, 6, 15, 17. Any four (4). 20
                                     ——
                                     20

12 Fabric identification

A *Gingham* – coloured warp/weft; plain weave.
B *Seerloop* – some slubbed yarns; plain weave.
C *Corduroy* – woven pile fabric; ribbed effect.
D *Vilene* – blended fibre; bonded fabric.
E *Jacquard jersey* – 'Fair Isle' effect on right side; knitted.
F *Laminated* – two layers; foam bonded; self lined; knitted.
G *Raschel* – warp knitted but not much 'give'; usually polyester fibre.
H *Tapestry weave* – colour woven; reversible.
I *Donegal tweed* – plain weave; white warp; coloured weft with coloured slubs.
J *Net* – transparent; yarns twisted to form mesh; no grain.
$(1 \times 10) - ((\frac{1}{2} \times 2) \times 10)$ 20
                                                    ——
                                                    20

13 Lace

(a) A Edging. (1)
B Eyelet. (1)
C Insertion. (1)
D Galloon. (1)
E Guipure. (1)   5

(b) A *Edging* – one straight edge; one shaped edge; various widths and colours; straight edge applied to garment. (2)
B *Eyelet* – two shaped edges; slits in centre for ribbon. (2)
C *Insertion* – two straight edges; woven pattern; twisted connecting threads. (2)
D *Galloon* – two shaped edges; heavy woven pattern; fine connecting threads. (2)
E *Guipure* – heavy motif; connecting bars; no mesh background. (2)   10

(c) A Neckline of a child's dress. (1)
B Shoulder strap of a nightdress. (1)
C Front panel of a blouse. (1)
D Lower edge of an underskirt. (1)
E Yoke line of a girl's dress. (1)   5
                    —
                    20

14 Narrow fabrics (1)

(a) A Broderie Anglaise edging – cotton. (2)
B Broderie Anglaise insertion – cotton. (2)
C Ric-rac braid – polyester, cotton or viscose. (2) 6

(b) A Plain weave; one raw edge; shaped holes punched and embroidered. (3)
B Plain weave; two shaped edges; oval holes for threading ribbon and embroidered motifs. (3)
C Braided; threads wound on bobbins and complicated plaiting method used. (2)   8

(c) A Hem edge of baby's dress. (1)
B Shoulder strap of nightdress. (1)
C Decoration on a girl's dress. (1)   3

(d) E.g. Paris binding, petersham, elastic, ribbon (1 mark for name and 2 marks for description.)   3
                    —
                    20

15 Narrow fabrics (2)

(a) A Bias-binding – cotton or nylon. (2)
B Embroidered ribbon – cotton, rayon, acrylic or nylon. (2)
C Fringe – cotton or rayon. (2)   6

(b) A Plain weave; cut on bias; edges folded to centre on wrong side. (3)
B Woven; two selvedges. (2)
C Woven edge; long 'z' twisted loops. (3)   8

(c) A Binding the armhole of a sleeveless dress. (1)
B Decorating a child's anorak. (1)
C Lamp shade. (1)   3

(d) Facing a curved edge; a casing for elastic at the waistline of a dress; narrow ties. (3)   3
                    —
                    20

16 Fabric properties (1)

Examples only:
(i) 2, 4, 6, 7, 10, 11. Any five (5).
(ii) 2, 5, 10, 11, 15, 18, 19, 20. Any five (5).
(iii) 6, 8, 9, 10, 13, 17. Any five (5).
(iv) 2, 3, 4, 6, 10, 14, 16. Any five (5).   20
                    —
                    20

17 Fabric properties (2)

(a) (i) Fibre or blend of fibres used, structure, weight, finish, design of garment, care. (6)
(ii) High flammability – cotton, linen, acrylic, acetate, viscose. (2)
   Low flammability – polyamide, polyester, wool, silk, Dicel, Darelle. (2)
   Good resistance to burning – modified acrylic, PVC, Nomex nylon. (2)   12

(b) (i) Relaxation, fibre swelling, felting. (3)
(ii) Temperature of setting must not be exceeded in dyeing, finishing or care. (3)
(iii) 1 Loss of shape; usually stretches (Acrilan/Orlon sweaters especially); knit a tension square before beginning and maintain even tension. (1)
   2 Seam shrinkage or gaps after washing; match thread and fabric type first and test. (1)   8
                    —
                    20

18 Fabric properties (3)

(a) (i) Tights, swimwear, foundation garments, ski wear. (3)

(ii) Helanca, Fluflon, Agilan. (3)

(iii) Lycra, Spanzelle. (1)

A core spun yarn is produced by twisting a fibrous sheath round the elastomeric fibre – so disguising it. (1)

(iv) A finish for cotton and cotton blends only. (1)

It gives a weft stretch only – a loosely woven cloth is passed through a solution of caustic soda under high tension in the warp direction, the fabric loses width. (5)   14

(b) Examples only: thickness/thinness; softness/harshness; stiffness/drape; smoothness/roughness. ($4 + \frac{1}{2}$ mark for each fabric to illustrate meaning)   6

                                                              —
                                                              20

19 Woven wool fabrics

A *Herringbone* (1) – twill weave; right and left twill; each section equal in width. (2)

B *Pick and pick* (1) – 2×2 twill; warp and weft yarns both alternate colours. (2)

C *Hopsack* (1) – plain weave; two threads used together in warp and weft. (1)

D *Barleycorn* (1) twill weave; barleycorn effect; warp and weft of contrasting colours. (2)

E *Dogtooth* (1) – twill weave; four light and four dark threads together in warp and weft. (2)

F *Two and two* (1) – 2×2 twill weave; two light and two dark threads in warp with a medium or dark contrasting weft. (2)

G *Glenurquhart check* (1) – twill weave, dark and light warp and weft combined to give check effect. (2)   20

                                                              —
                                                              20

4 Finishes

1 Trade names for fabric finishes

	Fibre type	Benefit
(i)	wool	non-shrink
(ii)	cotton, rayon	non-shrink
(iii)	cotton, rayon	crease resistant – non-iron, etc.
(iv)	nylon, polyester and other synthetics	resistance to static electicity
(v)	cotton, rayon	flame retardant
(vi)	wool	moth proof
(vii)	wool, cotton, rayon	water repellant
(viii)	wool, cotton, rayon	permanent pleats
(ix)	cotton	adds lustre
(x)	cotton, rayon, linen	adds lustre, more receptive to dyes

$$(2 \times 10) \quad \frac{20}{20}$$

2 Easy care finishes

(a) Good crease recovery; smooth drying; shape retention after washing; minimal or complete elimination of the need for ironing; easy to wash; quick to dry. (6)　　6
(b) Staining; soiling; static. (3)　　3
(c) Cotton, linen, viscose rayon. (2)　　2
(d) Acrylic, nylon, polyester (3); because they do not absorb water easily (they are hydrophobic) (1).　　4
(e) Careful choice of type of thread, trimmings, notions, lining and interfacing compatible with the easy care fabric. (5)　　5

$$\frac{}{20}$$

3 Mercerisation

John *Mercer* lived in *Accrington* (Lancashire) and in *1853* he discovered that if *cotton* fibres were steeped in a *caustic* soda *solution* they would *swell*. The ribbon like structure became *round*, but also shrank. If, however, the *yarns* were *stretched* and rinsed, they *retained* their original *length* and remained round. This process is widely used today on cotton fabrics, such as *poplin*, on sewing threads, such as *Sylko* and on embroidery *threads*, such as *stranded cotton*. This finish adds *lustre* and *increases* the *dye* affinity of the *fibres*.

$$(1 \times 20) \quad \frac{20}{20}$$

4 Plissé

Cotton *seersucker* is constructed using a *plain* weave, but the *warp* threads are grouped with alternately *tight* and loose *tension*. When the *fabric* is complete the characteristic *crinkled* effect is obtained.

The appearance of cotton *plissé* is very similar. To produce the same effect the plain *woven* cotton fabric is *printed* with a paste of *caustic* soda which causes the yarn to *shrink* in the printed areas. This produces a pucker in the *unprinted* areas.

Both fabrics *wash* well but should not be *ironed*. However, *seersucker* has a more lasting effect than *plissé*.

Nylon fabrics may also be produced with this effect and *phenol* is used in place of caustic *soda*.

$$(1 \times 20) \quad \frac{20}{20}$$

5 Static

(a) The friction (rubbing) of the fabric against itself, against the body or against another object. (3)   3

(b) Underskirts ride up, underskirts and dresses cling to legs, clothes 'spark' when taken off, dust and hairs are attracted and cling firmly. (4)   4

(c) Nylon. (1)   1

(d) Anti-static additives, introduced at the melt stage in manufacture, before fibre extrusion, provide a conducting layer on the fibre surface. (4)   4

(e) No special care is needed – wash or dry clean as indicated by the care label. (2)   2

(f) By adding a fabric softener to the final rinsing water. (2)   2

(g) E.g. underskirts, tights. (2)   2

(h) E.g. Lenor, Comfort. (2)   2

   —
   20

6 Permanent crease – Lintrak

(a) Lintrak. (1)

(b) International Wool Secretariat. (1)

(c) Trousers, skirts. (2)

(d) Wool, wool rich blends, cotton, linen, viscose. (2)

(e) Woven, knitted. (2)

(f) With a hand-held applicator. (1)

(g) Wrong side. (1)

(h) Silicon based resin. (2)

(i) To the inside of each crease. (1)

(j) It is turned to the right side and hung up, folded or laid flat. (2)

(k) The resin is self-curing. (1)

(l) The creases are resistant to washing and dry cleaning. (2)

(m) The natural crease resisting property of the wool is not affected. (2)

   20
   —
   20

7 Superwash wool (1)

(a) (i) International Wool Secretariat. (2)
(ii) Wool, wool blend. (2)   4

(b) The Woolmark or Woolblendmark must have been issued; it must be shrink resistant; fully machine washable; fast dye; quality controlled during manufacture. (5)   5

(c) (i) Early 1900s. (1)
(ii) Chlorine gas, chlorine and water solution. (2)
(iii) It softens the scales. (2)   5

(d) To enable the polymer to cling to the wool fibre. (2)   2

(e) No pre-treatment is necessary; applied to the finished garment or fabric rather than 'tops'; polymer does not encase the fibre but connects them with a very thin bridge. (4)   4

   —
   20

8 Superwash wool (2)

(a) (i) Diagram (Fig. 4.1) (2).
(ii) Protein fibre; overlapping scales (root to tip); highly resilient; natural crimp. (3)   5

(b) (i) A garment which has 'felted' would be – smaller than original size; harder to the touch; the fabric would be more compact. (3)
(ii) 'Felting' is caused by heat, moisture and friction, which in turn cause the fibre scales to overlap and lock into each other. (4)   7

(c) (i) Hercosett (1); the scales of the fibre are masked by coating them in a type of polyamide solution. (2) Diagram (Fig. 4.2) (1).
(ii) This can be carried out at most stages in manufacture, but most usually in the lap form after carding. (1)
(iii) Less likely to pill; more resistant to abrasion; warmer; still soft to handle. (3)   8

   —
   20

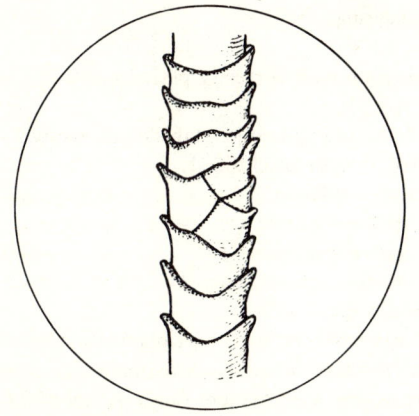

Fig. 4.1　Longitudinal section of a wool fibre.

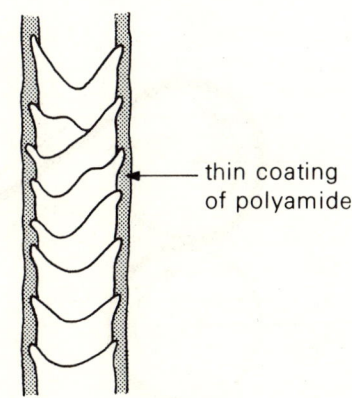

— thin coating of polyamide

Fig. 4.2　Scale-masking.

9　Moth proofing

(a)　Fig. 4.7　Beetle attack. (1)
　　　Fig. 4.8　Moth attack. (1)　　　　　　　　　2
(b)　Wool, camel hair, mohair, cashmere, etc. (3)　3
(c)　Dark places; undisturbed; dirty clothes; upholstery; carpets, especially carpets under heavy furniture which is rarely moved. (2)　　　　　　　　　2
(d)　(i) Dielmoth – contact insecticide. (2)
　　　Eulan – insect stomach poison. (2)
　　　Mitin FF – insect stomach poison. (2)
　　　(ii) Eulan and Mitin FF. (2)
　　　(iii) Toxicity. (1)　　　　　　　　　　　　9
(e)　During dyeing, printing or setting. (1)　　　1
(f)　Make sure it is clean; pack in a polythene bag, place vapourised strip or mothballs near the jumper; inspect it regularly. (3)　　　　　　3
　　　　　　　　　　　　　　　　　　　　　　　——
　　　　　　　　　　　　　　　　　　　　　　　20

10　Showerproofing

(a)　Wool gaberdine. (1)　　　　　　　　　　　1
(b)　Wool. (1)　　　　　　　　　　　　　　　1
(c)　To treat (1) a fabric (1) in order to delay (1) the absorption (1) and penetration (1) of water (1); the fabric remains permeable (1) to air (1).　　　8
(d)　(i) Charles Macintosh. (1)
　　　(ii) A waterproof coat is still called a mackintosh, mac or pak-a-mac. (1)
　　　(iii) Linseed oil – oil skins. (2)
　　　Pitch and wax – tarpaulins, canvas roofing. (2)
　　　PVC coated cottons – aprons, coats. (2)　8
(e)　Water repellant. (1)　　　　　　　　　　1
(f)　Silicones. (1)　　　　　　　　　　　　　1
　　　　　　　　　　　　　　　　　　　　　　　——
　　　　　　　　　　　　　　　　　　　　　　　20

11 Flame-retardant finishes (1)

(a) Proban X, Provartex CP. (2) 2
(b) Cotton, linen, viscose rayon. (3) 3
(c) Fabric weight; construction; end uses. (3) 3
(d) Suppress release of flammable tars (2); induces carbonisation so the fabric is self extinguishing (2); prevents fabric flaring up (1). 5
(e) Wash and dry clean according to instructions on label; do not bleach. (5) 5
(f) Cellular blankets, bedspreads, curtains, chair covers, etc. ($\frac{1}{2} \times 4$) 2
—
20

12 Flame-retardant finishes (2)

(a) Wool. (1) 1
(b) It smoulders and chars. (2) 2
(c) Contains high percentage of nitrogen; has a high ignition temperature; has a low heat of combustion; is an absorbent fibre and so contains a high percentage of moisture. (4) 4
(d) For use in public places; use in buildings, etc., where central heating causes the wool to be unnaturally dry. (2) 2
(e) During dyeing. (1) 1
(f) International Wool Secretariat. (1) 1
(g) Mohair, angora, camel hair. (1) 1
(h) Moth proofing, Superwash, water repellancy. (3) 3
(i) *Protective clothing* – in steel, car and chemical industries.
Railways – seat covers, curtains, carpets.
Aircraft – upholstery, blankets, uniforms, carpets, curtains.
Hotels – upholstery, blankets, wall coverings, carpets, curtains.
($\frac{1}{2} \times 10$) 5
—
20

13 Calendering

(a) (i) Diagram with correctly placed arrows (Fig. 4.3) (4).
(ii) Metal and soft rollers labelled correctly. (3)
(iii) Solid paper or cloth. (1)
(iv) Metal rollers. (1)
(v) 1 *ironed* – simple. (1)
   2 *glazed* – friction. (1)
   3 *lustre* – schreinering. (1)
(vi) Resin. (1) 13
(b) (i) Moiré has been used on ribbed silk fabrics for over 200 years. Since the development of *acetate* moiré is now a permanent finish. A *ribbed* fabric is essential as the calender is *smooth*. Two layers of fabric are placed on top of each other slightly off grain. The two layers are stitched together on the selvedges and fed through the *heated* metal calender rollers. *Heavy* pressure causes the rib pattern of the two layers to press onto each other and so *flatten* certain ribbed areas. (6)
(ii) Water marked. (1) 7
—
20

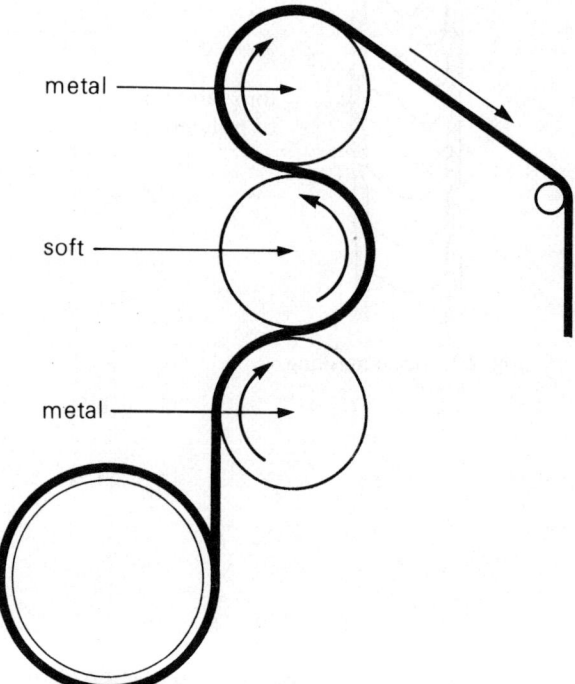

Fig. 4.3 A calender.

14 Raising

(a) (Fig. 4.4) Fabric (1) – direction (1).
    P (1) – hooks (1) – direction (1).
    CP (1) – hooks (1) – direction (1).   8
(b) Teasel (1); tall plant, large prickly head (1).   2
(c) Warmth – fibres on surface trap air which is a
    good insulator. (2)
    Softness – the fabric feels very soft although it may
    be weaker. (2)
    Appearance – gives a dull surface and a thicker
    looking fabric. (2)
    Repellance of water and stains – fibre ends on the
    surface cut down the rapidity with which the fabric
    gets wet. (2)   8
(d) Blankets, flannelette, melton, winceyette, beaver
    cloth, brushed denim etc. (2)   2
                                                          ──
                                                          20

15 Sanforisation

(a) A thick, felt blanket with the damp fabric clinging
    to its surface, passes around the guide roller. In
    this curved position the outer surface stretches and
    the inner one contracts. The heated metal shoe
    holds the fabric firmly against the blanket so that
    when the blanket straightens out the fabric is
    shrunk accordingly. The fabric is then dried as it
    passes the heated dryer.   16
(b) Cotton poplin, linen lawn, slub weave, viscose
    rayon. (3)   3
(c) Rigmel. (1)   1
                                                          ──
                                                          20

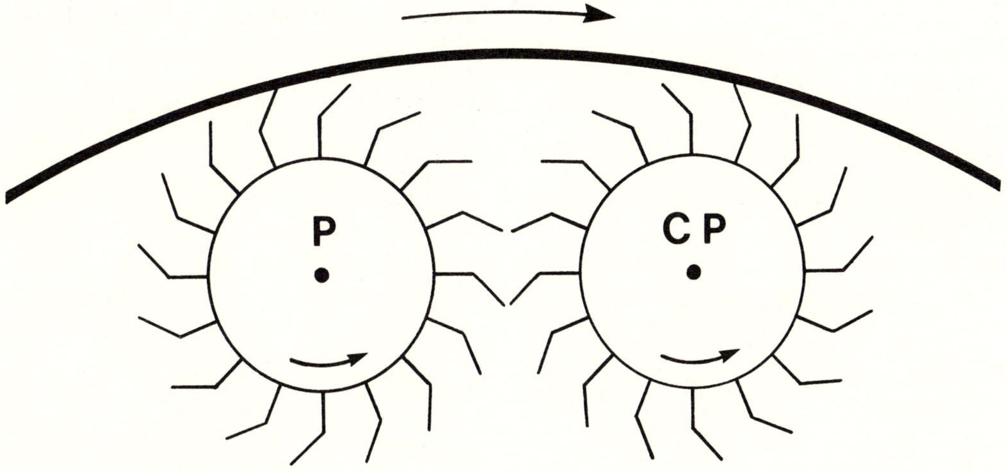

Fig. 4.4 A raising machine.

16 Mechanical finishing – stenter drying

(a) (i) To recover width lost in processing. (2)
(ii) By pins or clips. (2)
(iii) The width between the pins is increased; hot air is blown over and under the fabric; the weft yarns are pulled to make sure thay are at right angles to the warp threads. (4)
(iv) The width of the fabric is correct and even, the fabric is crease free and dry. (3)
(v) The holes of the stentering pins remain in the fabric at the selvedges. (1)   12
(b) Resins – for crease resistance. (2)   2
(c) Fabric subjected to a temperature approaching the softening point of the fibre while held in the stenter. (3)   3
(d) Sanforising, calendering, raising. (3)   3
    —
    20

17 Specialised finishes

Beetling
Linen (1) – the fabric is dampened and fed through a machine which beats the fabric with wooden hammers. The result is a closer, more compact weave and a slightly lustrous surface to the fabric (4).

Decatizing
Worsted (wool) (1) – the fabric is wound tightly onto a perforated roller and steam is blown through it. The handle and appearance of the fabric is improved (4).

Gassing
Cottons and silk (1) – this is a pre-treatment to bleaching and finishing to remove unwanted surface hairs or filaments produced in manufacture. The unwanted fibres are removed by passing through a flame or are burnt off by a hot-plate. The result is a smoother fabric (4).

Weighting
Silk (1) – tin salts are applied to increase the weight. The treatment also modifies the handle and appearance of the fabric. If too much weighting is added the fabric will crack and wear badly (4).
    20
    —
    20

5 Colour

1 Colours

(a) Red, yellow, blue. ($1\frac{1}{2}$) $1\frac{1}{2}$

(b) Orange, green, purple. ($1\frac{1}{2}$) $1\frac{1}{2}$

(c) Purple/orange, orange/green, purple/green. ($1\frac{1}{2}$) $1\frac{1}{2}$

(d) Red – green, yellow – purple, blue – orange. ($1\frac{1}{2}$) $1\frac{1}{2}$

(e) By mixing two colours to obtain another colour, e.g. red and yellow to get orange. (2) 2

(f) Black added to a colour. (2) 2

(g) White added to a colour. (2) 2

(h) All one colour. (1) 1

(i) Shades and tints. (1) 1

(j) Colours joining each other in the colour circle; colours looking brighter together; the edges of these colours merge and they look alike from a distance. (3) 3

(k) Colours of equal value; colours opposite each other in the colour circle; when mixed they make grey. (3) 3

—

20

2 Tie dye and batik

(a) (i) A Elastic bands. (1)

B Thread (stitched). (1)

C A cork. (1)

D Pegs. (1)

E String. (1) 5

(ii) Stitched method. (1) 1

(iii) Instructions to include: preparation of the fabric (2); preparation of the dye (1); finishing (1). 4

(b) *Batik* is a form of craft dyeing which originated in *Indonesia*, in which *wax* or *starch* are used to *resist* the dye and build up a pattern. Beautiful *designs* can be achieved by applying wax when the fabric is dry and then dyeing in a *darker* shade. Finally the wax must be removed by *boiling* or by *ironing* between sheets of *newspaper*. (10) 10

—

20

3 Colour fastness

(a) (i) Towels – water too hot; colour comes loose in water. (2)

(ii) Jeans – at knees and hemlines; fibres worn and colour fades. (2)

(iii) Blouse – underarm; acidity in perspiration reduces the colour. (2)

(iv) Lining of skirt – blue goes purple; but returns to normal on cooling. (2)

(v) Swimming costume – salt leaves deposits which reduce the colour if not rinsed out. (2) 10

(b) Excess dye comes away on the first wash. (1) 1

(c) Salt in the rinsing water. (2) 2

(d) Place piece of white cloth on inside of section of hem – cover with a damp cloth – see if colour comes off on white cloth when pressed. (3) 3

(e) A chemical additive used to bind the dye to a fibre that would not otherwise take it, e.g. ammonium sulphate. (4) 4

—

20

4 Dyes

(a) (i) Wool, silk. (2)

(ii) Cotton, rayon. (2)

(iii) Nylon, wool. (2)

(iv) Nylon, polyester, acrylic, triacetates. (2) 8

(b) Solution dyed before extrusion. (2) 2

(c) A mixture fabric woven of warp and weft threads with different dye affinity, e.g. viscose/acetate lining. (4) 4

(d) Different colours show when viewed from various angles – warp/weft different colours – an example of cross dyeing. (3) 3

(e) Used in manufacture of synthetic filaments for identification during manufacture only – colour later washed out. (3) 3

—

20

5 Home dyeing

(a) Nylon, polyester. (2)   2
(b) Acrylic. (1)   1
(c) Wool, cotton. (2)   2
(d) Salt, soda or Dye Fix. (2)   2
(e) Clean article; make sure no repairs are needed;
    know the fibre content of the garment or fabric;
    know the dry weight of the garment or fabric; use
    a container large enough to keep the garment
    submerged and moving; dissolve correct quantity
    of dye; maintain solution at the correct
    temperature; wet garment thoroughly; keep
    garment submerged and moving; time dyeing pro-
    cess; rinse thoroughly to remove loose dye. (12)   12
(f) Home dye remover. (1)   1
                                                                    —
                                                                    20

6 Colour in fabrics

(a) Fibre, yarn, fabric. (3)   3
(b) After weaving. (1)   1
(c) Unravel the fabric and examine the yarn. (2)   2
(d) Weft threads (1); tartan, gingham. (2)   3
(e) Pattern on the straight grain; fabric reversible. (2) 2
(f) Fair Isle. (1)   1
(g) Jacquard. (1)   1
(h) Fig. 5.2 knitting – 3 colours. (2)
    Fig. 5.3 weaving – 2 colours. (2)   4
(i) (i) Shot, twill. (1)
    (ii) Stripe. (1)
    (iii) Check. (1)   3
                                                                    —
                                                                    20

7 Roller printing

A Printing roller (1) – engraved; copper; one per
colour (3).
B Grey cloth – not printed. (1)
C Printed cloth. (1)
D Colour roller (1) – picks up colour from the tank
below. (2)
E Tank (1) – contains the colour. (1)
F Doctor blades (1) – one each side of the colour
roller; one to remove surplus colour, the other to
remove fluff from the fabric which would otherwise
cause imperfect prints. (5)
G Drum (1) – fabric rolls round the drum; right side
fabric to printing roller. (2)   20
                                                        —
                                                        20

8 Variations of roller printing

Duplex – both sides are printed simultaneously. (2)
Resist – the fabric is first printed with chemicals which
resist the dye; a white pattern on a coloured ground is
obtained. (4)
Discharge – the fabric is first dyed and then printed
with chemicals which remove the dye from the
patterned areas; it is used for fabrics with a light
pattern on a dark background; right side and wrong
side of fabric alike. (5)
Transfer – relatively new method; the design is first
printed onto paper and then transferred to the fabric;
it can be used on woven and knitted fabrics and on
garments. (5)
Flock – the fabric design is printed on with a sticky
substance; very short fibres are then sprinkled on.
These stick to the fabric and cause the raised
design. (4)   20
                                                        —
                                                        20

9 Block, screen and roller printing

Hand block – e.g. lino block; pattern marked on and
the background is removed – the design is left in
relief. (5)
Roller printing – by machine; design engraved on
rollers made of copper, background left plain –
originally done by hand. (7)
Screen printing – by hand or machine; a screen the size
of the design is prepared of nylon or silk gauze; the
background is painted out with shellac; may be
photographically produced; dye paste is pressed
through the gauze with a squeegee. (8)   20
                                                        —
                                                        20

10 Metameric effect

(a) Sunlight or daylight – some dyes fade after long exposure. (2)

Fluorescent – supposed to simulate daylight so no change in colour. (2)

Sodium – appears to be considerable colour change. (2)   6

(b) and (c) Collect four different coloured cotton poplin or printed fabrics; mount them as described on p. 62; take them into fluorescent light and sodium light and make a note of any apparent colour change; expose them to the sunlight for two months and complete the table of results. (6 + 8)   14

      —

     20

11 Speciality woollens

(a) (i) Rough feel; hard wearing. (2)

(ii) Coloured weft threads instead of white; variety in weights. (2)   4

(b) (i) No wrong side. (1)

(ii) Garment can be made reversible; very warm. (2)   3

(c) (i) 70 cm (1); rough, hairy surface. (2)

(ii) Examples only:

Black Watch – green, black, navy.

Dress Stewart – white, red, black, yellow.

Mackenzie – green, navy, red, white.

Gordon – blue, black, green, yellow.

(1 mark for each name, 2 marks for description)   9

(d) Fig. 5.6.

(i) Orb – Harris Tweed. (1)

(ii) Thistle – pure new wool woven in Scotland – Scottish tartan. (1)

(iii) Dragon – Welsh Woollens Mark – Welsh flannel. (1)

(iv) Crook and flag – British Wool. (1)   4

      —

     20

HARRIS TWEED

(i)

(ii)

(iii)

(iv)

Fig. 5.1

6 Care

1 Sportswear

(a) (i) Rinse costume in clean water (1) immediately (1). When you get home wash and rinse costume and towel (1) according to instructions (1). Dry thoroughly and air properly (1).   5

(ii) Remove any stains, e.g. grass (1). Wash according to instructions (1) and iron (1). Remove dirty marks and stains from plimsolls (1). Clean with appropriate cleaner (1).   5

(iii) Wash whole kit each time used (1). Press (1). Remove mud from boots and clean studs (1). Preserve leather boots with dubbin (1).   4

(b) Cost will vary according to quality and type of equipment, but the prices quoted should be realistic. (2 × 3)   6

—
20

2 School clothes (1)

(a) (i) Brush and remove fluff, etc. (1). Hang up (1).   2

(ii) Empty pockets (1). Check for small repairs (1). Wash and press (1). Hang up (1).   4

(iii) Check for larger repairs and alterations to size (1). Wash and press (1). Hang up in wardrobe or cover with plastic bag (1).   3

(b) (i) Diagram (Fig. 6.1) (5).   5

(ii) Warm (160°C).   1

(c) (i) Mark position with two pins;

(ii) use single, matching thread and stab stitch 6 stitches through holes and over pins;

(iii) remove pins and take thread to right side;

(iv) twist thread round stitches 4 times;

(v) take thread to wrong side and loop stitch over stitches on wrong side. Fasten off firmly. (5)   5

—
20

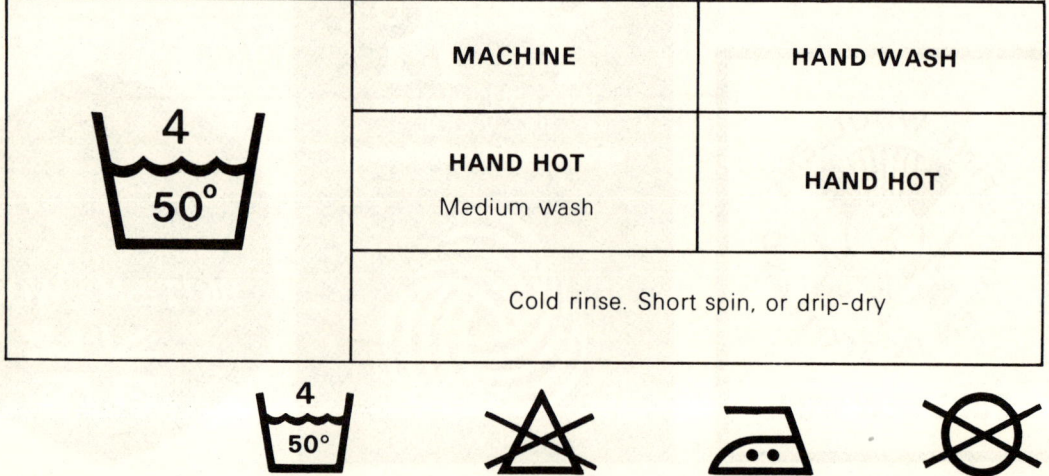

Fig. 6.1   A care label on a blouse or a shirt of polyester/cotton poplin.

3 School clothes (2)

(a) Thin place darn (Fig. 6.2) (1) – match thread for colour and texture (1); work on wrong side covering thin place and surrounding worn parts (1); pick up and pass each thread alternately (1); leave short ends; do not fasten off (1). 5

Patch (1) – bought patch of fabric, suede or soft PVC; own choice of fabric to suit jumper (1); prepare edges if necessary, turn in a narrow turning to make curved ends rather than square corners (1); place carefully, covering well over the thin places (1); stab stitch a little way in from the edge (1). 5

(b) Allow 5 mm at each end for turning under if possible; fold under ends and tack in position on double fabric; start on one long side and hem neatly; one stitch at each corner (Fig. 6.3). (4) 4

(c) Remove any stains (1). Wash according to wash code 4 (1). 2

(d) Remove fluff, hairs and dust daily (1). Do not put too much in pockets (1). Hang up on coathanger when not being worn (1). Sponge off marks as they occur; dry clean or wash according to the care label (1). 4

——
20

4 Underwear

(a) Easier to clean lightly soiled garments (1); clothes last longer (1); more pleasant to wear clean underclothes (1). 3

(b) Whether it will wash (1); colour fast (1); correct size (1); type of fabric suitable to be worn next to the skin (1); nylon garments – anti-stat finish (1); good quality and value for money (1). 6

(c) Undo the seam (1). Check that the knitted fabric has not worn (1). Re-stitch the seam with overlock stitch or 3 step zig-zag. Press (1). 3

(d) Add frill (1) or lace (1). 2

Frill – use matching, toning or contrasting colour of similar fabric (1); cut fabric twice the length of the lower edge of the underskirt (1); neaten lower edge (1) and gather top edge (1); attach to the underskirt (1) and neaten the seam (1).

Lace – width equal to extra length needed (1); equal length plus 2 cm turnings or allow for gathering (1); join to right side of underskirt by machine or embroidery stitch (1); to join the lace, overlap the ends so that the pattern joins; work running stitch or machine stitch around design and satin stitch over the straight stitching; trim excess lace close to satin stitch on right side and wrong side (3). 6

——
20

Fig. 6.2 A thin place darn.

Fig. 6.3 Attaching a name tape.

(i) Cut a piece of 1 cm wide tape 6 cm long. Turn under 1 cm at each end of the tape. Tack the loop to the centre back of the back of the coat, leaving a little bit of slack tape. Hem round the three outside edges and back stitch across the inside edges. (Fig. 6.4) (5)   5

(ii) Cut a patch large enough to cover the hole and any worn part. Turn 1 cm to wrong side all round. Mitre corners. Tack the patch over hole on right side, matching straight grain. Machine close to the edge on the right side, overlapping the stitching at start and finish for strength. Trim the edges level on wrong side and loop stitch to neaten. A second line of machining can be worked on the right side to match with any other seam stitching on the jeans. (Fig. 6.5) (7)   7

(iii) Remove frayed threads and fasten off ends of existing stitching. Turn under the raw edges and tack the hem in position; slip hem; remove tackings and press. (Fig. 6.6) (4)   4

(iv) Undo any weak stitching. Tack the seam together on the fitting line. Match the thread with the garment. Machine or back stitch on the fitting line. Overlap previous stitching at the start and finish. Remove the tackings and press the seam open. (Fig. 6.7) (4)   4

———
20

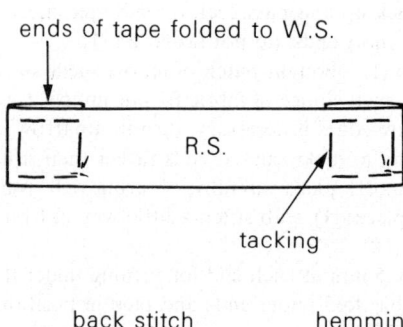

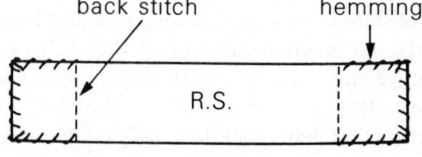

Fig. 6.4   Repairing a broken hanging loop.

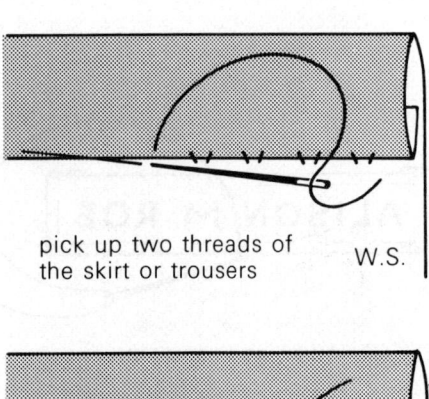

pick up two threads of the skirt or trousers   W.S.

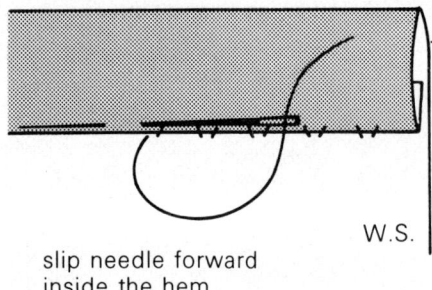

slip needle forward inside the hem

Fig. 6.6   Repairing a hem.

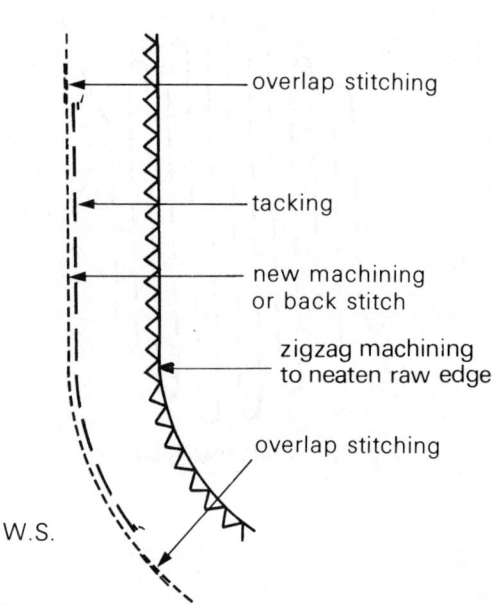

Fig. 6.7   Repairing a split seam.

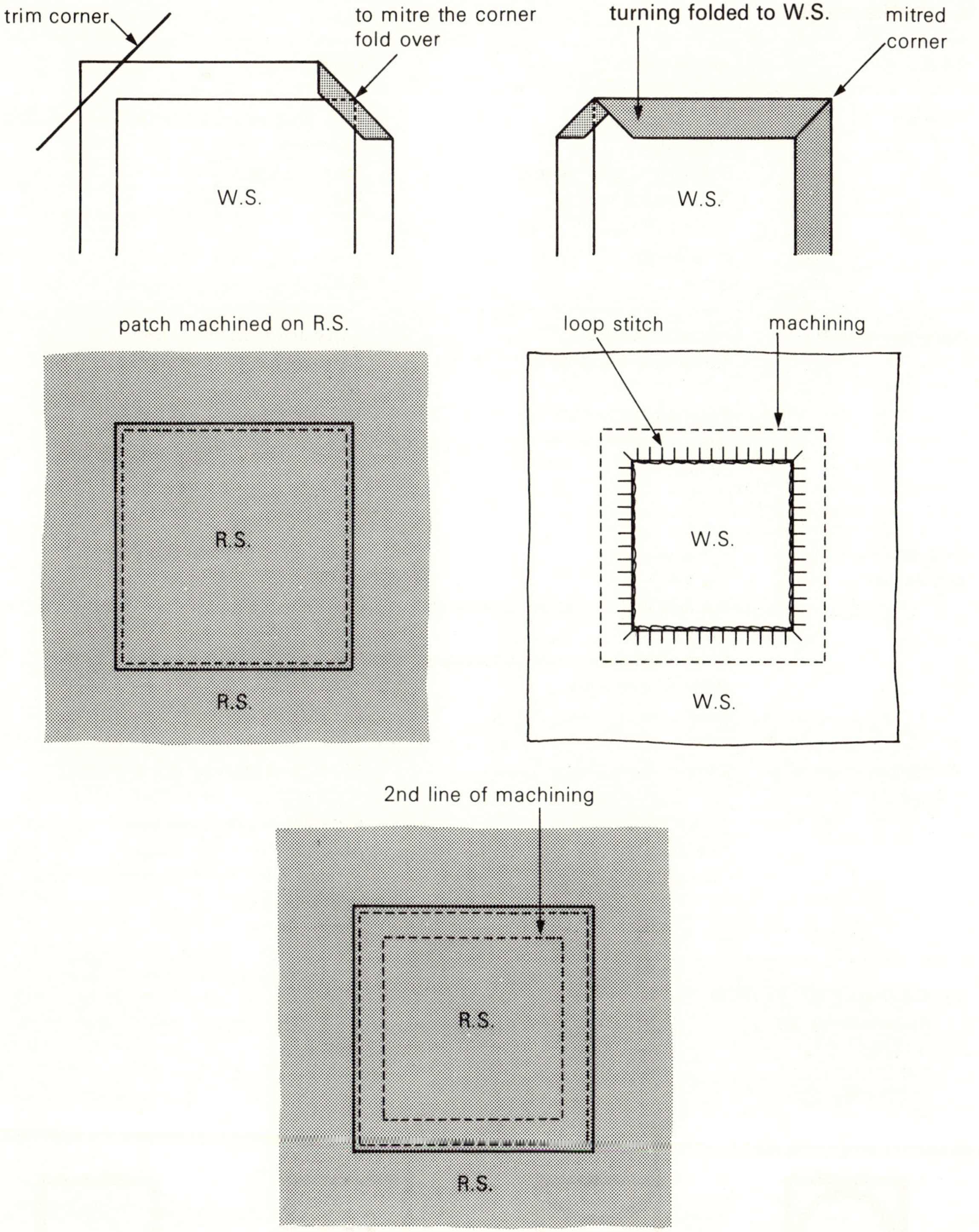

trim corner

to mitre the corner
fold over

W.S.

turning folded to W.S.

mitred corner

W.S.

patch machined on R.S.

R.S.

R.S.

loop stitch

machining

W.S.

W.S.

2nd line of machining

R.S.

R.S.

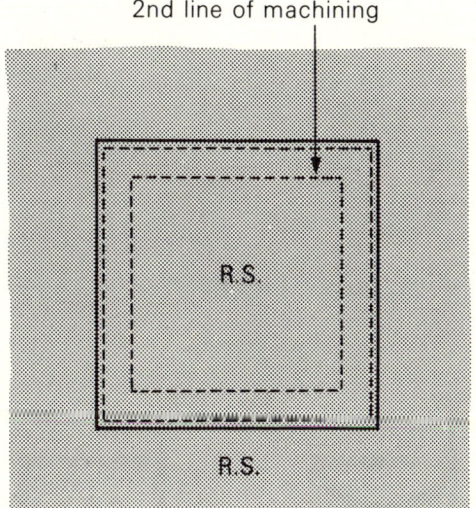

Fig. 6.5   Repairing a hole in the knee of a pair of jeans.

6 Washing machines

Type	Advantages	Disadvantages
Automatic (1)	Easy to use Time saver No physical effort needed No attention needed Correct treatment for fabrics on correct programme ($\frac{1}{2} \times 3$)	Each programme takes quite a bit of time Expensive Takes up space Uses a lot of water ($\frac{1}{2} \times 3$)
Semi-automatic (1)	Not so expensive No physical effort needed Large for big loads Small amounts can be done more easily on own ($\frac{1}{2} \times 3$)	Large and takes up space Someone has to be available to alter switches Not moveable ($\frac{1}{2} \times 3$)
Twin-tub washing machine (1)	Range of prices Washing and rinsing are quickly and easily done More convenient for small amounts Quite easy to move ($\frac{1}{2} \times 3$)	Needs more physical effort Tub and spin drier rather small Needs more attention while washing ($\frac{1}{2} \times 3$)
Washing machine with wringer (1)	Comparatively cheap Variety of sizes Not too large Moveable ($\frac{1}{2} \times 3$)	Much more physical effort needed Constant attention required May not have water heater Wringer tends to be harder on clothes than spin drier ($\frac{1}{2} \times 3$)

(b) Diagrams (Fig. 6.8). ($\frac{1}{2} \times 4$)   16
    (i) Tumble dry. ($\frac{1}{2}$)
    (ii) Line dry. ($\frac{1}{2}$)
    (iii) Drip dry. ($\frac{1}{2}$)
    (iv) Dry flat. ($\frac{1}{2}$)   4
                                                          —
                                                          20

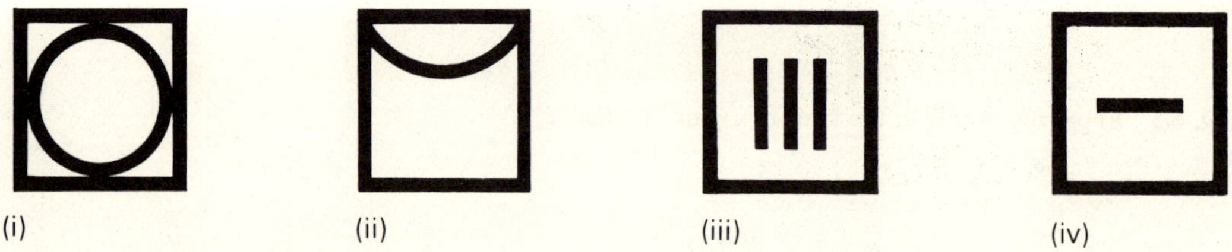

(i)   (ii)   (iii)   (iv)

Fig. 6.8 Drying clothes symbols.

7 Laundering clothes

(**a**)

Advantages	Disadvantages
(i) e.g. convenient, cheaper (2)	time needed, space needed for equipment, equipment has to be bought (2)
(ii) e.g. no mess at home, not too expensive, can meet people (2)	transport needed, time needed (2)
(iii) e.g. very convenient if busy or unable to do washing, good finish, ready to put away (2)	expensive, extra clothes needed because of time taken, may lose clothes, wears clothes out more quickly (2)

12

(b) Examples only:
Stain softener – to spray on stains or soiled area before washing, e.g. Frend.
Fabric softener – used in final rinse, e.g. Comfort.
Starch – used to stiffen.
Soapless detergent – used for washing, e.g. Daz.
Biological powder – used for removing stains during washing, e.g. Bold.
Iron cleaner – used to clean surface of sole plate of iron, e.g. iron cleaner by Vilene.
(Products 1 × 4; how used 1 × 4)   8

——
20

8 Methods of laundering clothes

(a) (i) Launderette (1) – little room for drying in a flat; can share cost with other students; no expensive equipment needed; detergent available as required instead of having to buy packets. (3)
(ii) Automatic or semi-automatic washer (1) – time valuable for mother with small children; a lot of washing of similar fabrics; expensive, but a long term investment. (3)
(iii) Small washing machine and spin drier (1) – not so much washing; small amounts to be done at any one time; spin drier very useful for washing done by hand; not too expensive; economic to use. (3) 12
(b) Iron, ironing board, washing machine, laundry basket, clothes line, pegs, airer, etc. ($\frac{1}{2}$ × 8); costs may vary but should be realistic ($\frac{1}{2}$ × 8).   8

——
20

9 Laundry aids

(a)

Hard soap	Soap powder
Fairy	Persil
Palmolive	

Soapless detergent	Liquid detergent
Dreft	Stergene
Surf	Dynamo
Daz	Woolite

Biological powder	Fabric softener
Bold	Lenor
Ariel	Comfort
	Softlan

Fabric finish	Soap flakes
Finish	Lux
Fabulon	

Fabric stiffener	Stain softener
Starch	Shout
	Frend

($\frac{1}{2}$ × 20)   10

(b) Price from each store; comparison, taking into account the packet size. (2 × 5)   10

——
20

10 Care symbols (1)

(a) International Care Labelling Code. (4)   4
(b) (i) For washing by hand or by machine. (2)
(ii) For bleaching. (2)
(iii) For ironing. (2)
(iv) For dry cleaning. (2)   8
(c) No need to identify fabrics (1); sorting and washing is easier (1).   2
(d) i (e) ii (f) iv (g) iii (h) iii (i) ii. (6)   6

——
20

11 Care symbols (2)

(a) (Fig. 6.9)
  (i) Diagram. (3)
  Blouse ($\frac{1}{2}$) – silk (1) – any colour ($\frac{1}{2}$).   5
  (ii) Diagram. (3)
  Shirt ($\frac{1}{2}$) – polyester/cotton (1) – most colours (if fast) ($\frac{1}{2}$).   5
  (iii) Diagram. (3).
  Jumper ($\frac{1}{2}$) – acrylic (1) – most colours ($\frac{1}{2}$).   5
(b) (i) Cool 120°C. (1)
  (ii) Warm 160°C. (1)
  (iii) Hot 210°C. (1)   3
(c) Do not iron, as ironing would spoil the fabric. (2) 2
  —
  20

12 Care symbols (3)

(a) (Fig. 6.10)
  (i) Diagram (3).
  Jumper ($\frac{1}{2}$) – wool (1) – any colour ($\frac{1}{2}$).   5
  (ii) Diagram (3).
  Towel ($\frac{1}{2}$) – cotton towelling (1) – fast colours ($\frac{1}{2}$). 5
  (iii) Diagram (3).
  Socks ($\frac{1}{2}$) – nylon (1) – white ($\frac{1}{2}$).   5
(b) (i) Do not wash. (1)
  (ii) Do not bleach. (1)
  (iii) Chlorine bleach may be used (1)   3
(c) Garment should be hand washed – 40°C. (2)   2
  —
  20

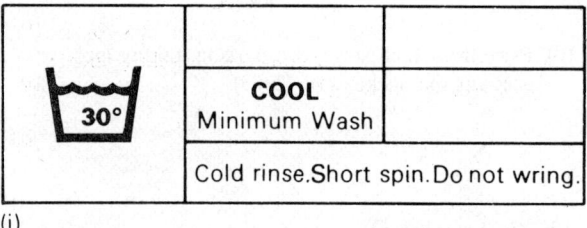

(i)

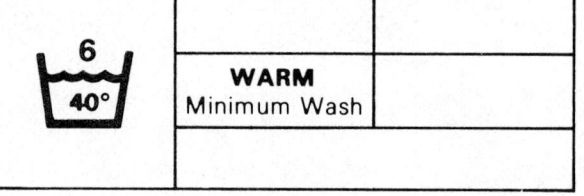

(ii)

6 40° WARM Minimum Wash

(iii)

Fig. 6.9

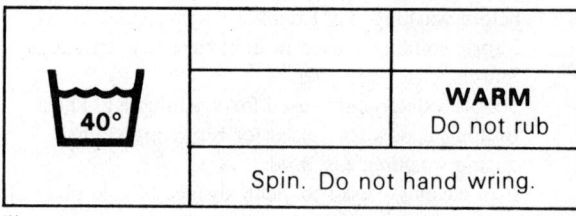

(i)

2 HOT Maximum Wash HAND HOT

(ii)

60° HAND HOT Cold rinse. Short spin or drip dry.

(iii)

Fig. 6.10

13 Care symbols (4)

(a) (Fig. 6.11)
    (i) Diagram (3).
    Sheets ($\frac{1}{2}$) – cotton (1) – white ($\frac{1}{2}$).   5
    (ii) Diagram (3).
    Blouse ($\frac{1}{2}$) – rayon (1) – colour fast in warm
    water ($\frac{1}{2}$)   5
    (iii) Diagram (3).
    Skirt ($\frac{1}{2}$) – cotton (1) – white ($\frac{1}{2}$).   5
(b) It is used for cotton articles which have a special
    finish enabling them to be boiled, but they only
    need drip-drying. (5)   5
    —
    20

14 Garment label

(i) 1 Manufacturer's registered trade mark. (2)
    2 Country of origin. (1)
    3 British sizing. (1)
    4 European sizing. (1)
    5 Bust size in centimetres and inches. (1)
    6 Fibre content. (1)
    7 Washing code 4, water temperature 50°C. (4)
    8 Dry flat. (2)
    9 Cool iron. (2)
   10 Can be dry cleaned in perchlorethylene, white
     spirit, solvent 113 and solvent 11. (3)
   11 Special washing instructions. (1)
   12 Manufacturer's reference number. (1)ı   20
    —
    20

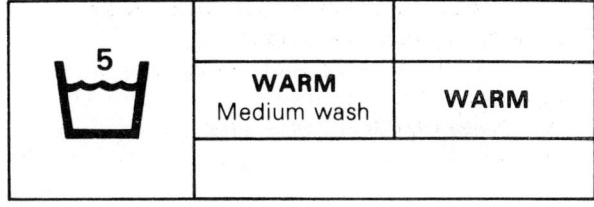

(i)

(ii)

(iii)
Fig. 6.11

15 Ball-band

  1 Size of crochet hook to be used – United Kingdom,
    United States and Continental sizes. (2)
  2 Size of knitting needle to be used – United
    Kingdom, United States and Continental sizes. (2)
  3 Washing code, water to be 40°C. (2)
  4 Temperature of the iron – cool 120°C. (2)
  5 Can be dry cleaned in all solvents. (2)
  6 Do not bleach. (2)
  7 Colour number for matching. (2)
  8 Dye number for matching. (2)
  9 British Standard's number, to which all knitting
    yarns must comply for quality. (1)
 10 Four strands twisted together. (2)   20
    —
    20

16 Stain removal

(i)   Egg, blood – most washable fabrics. (2)

(ii) Ink – most washable fabrics. (2)

(iii) Iron mould, rust – all white fabrics. (2)

(iv) Coffee, fruit juices, tea – wool, silk, rayons, synthetics. (2)

(v)   Ball point pen, grass – most fabrics – test first. (2)

(vi) Paint, varnish – most fabrics. (2)

(vii) Lipstick – wool, silk, rayons, synthetics. (2)

(viii)Chewing gum – most fabrics. (2)

(ix) Nail varnish – most fabrics, except acetate rayon. (2)

(x)   Perspiration, beer – most fabrics – test rayons first. (2)   20
                                                                                     —
                                                                                    20

17 Dry cleaning

(a) Check that buttons are safe for cleaning (1). Make sure garment is in good repair (1). Empty pockets and remove metal badges (1). Take to the cleaners any special treatment ticket applying to the garment (1). Point out stains to assistant in the shop (1).   5

(b) Association of British Launderers and Cleaners. (4)   4

(c) (i) Goods normal for dry cleaning in all solvents. (1)
    (ii) Goods normal for dry cleaning in perchlorethylene, white spirit, solvent 113 and solvent 11. (3)
    (iii) Goods normal for dry cleaning in white spirit or solvent 113. (2)   6

(d) The garment must not be dry cleaned. (1)   1

(e) (i) Check for loose buttons, leather trims, etc. and remove these;
    (ii) read operating instructions carefully;
    (iii) weigh the clothes;
    (iv) 'spot' bad stains;
    (v) make sure the door is shut properly after the garments have been put in;
    (vi) insert coins;
    (vii) hang or press after removal from machine;
    (viii) air well. $(\frac{1}{2} \times 8)$ 4
                                                                    —
                                                                   20

7 Solutions to word searches and crosswords

Word search – fibres

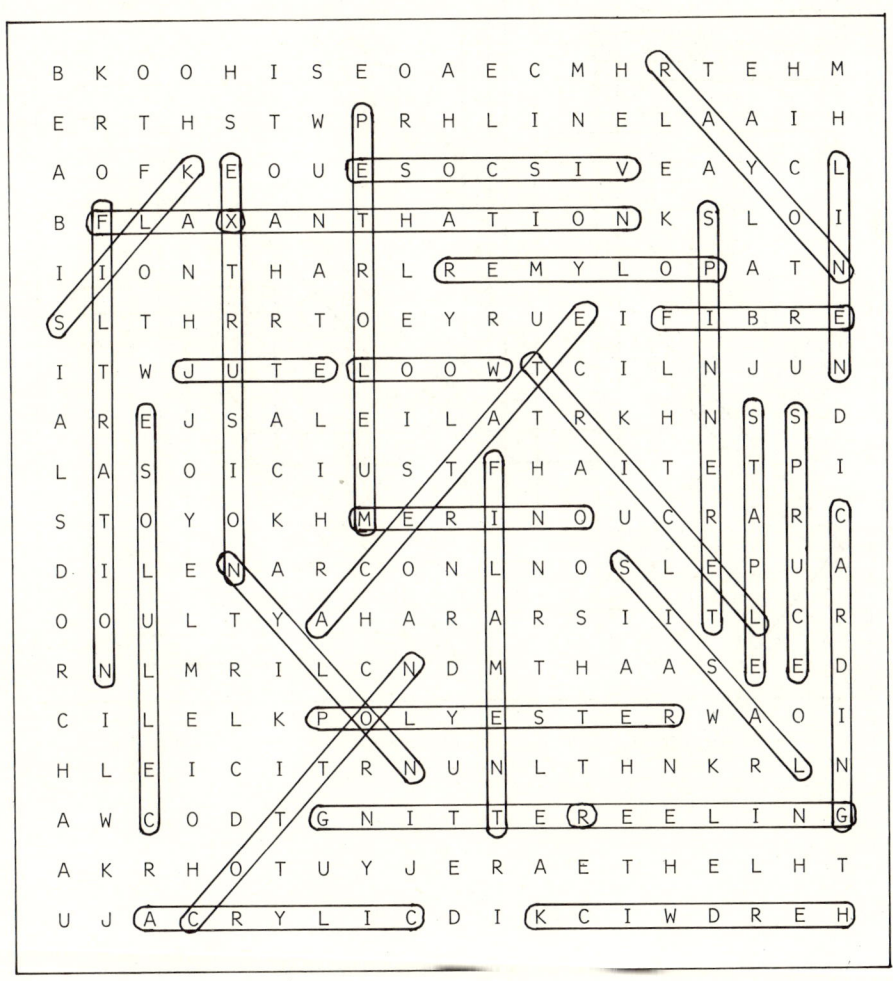

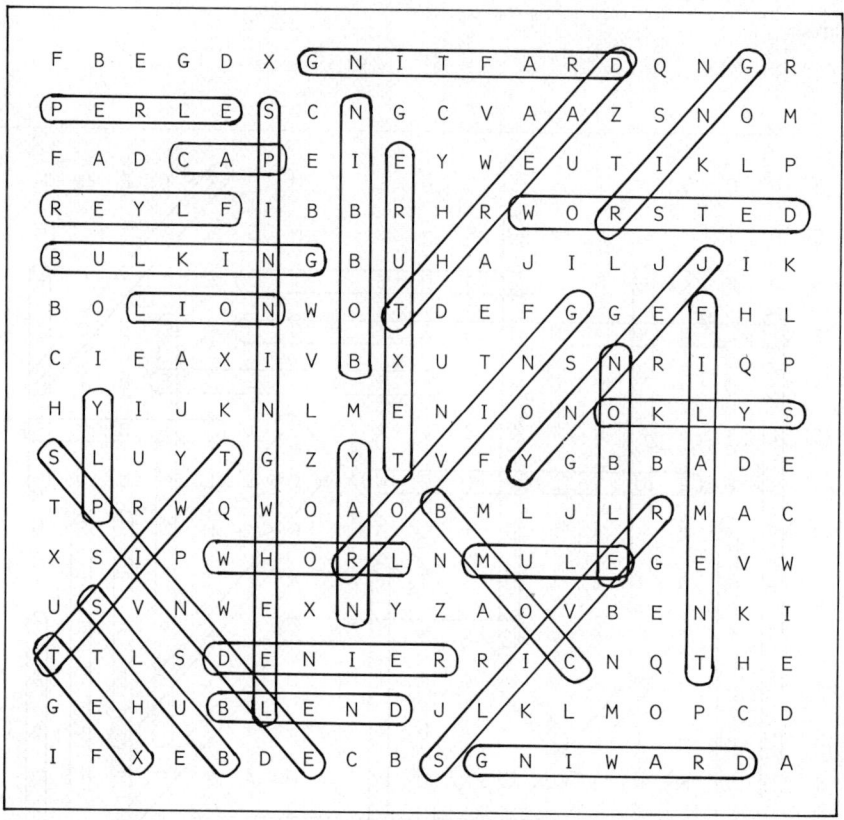

Word search – fabrics

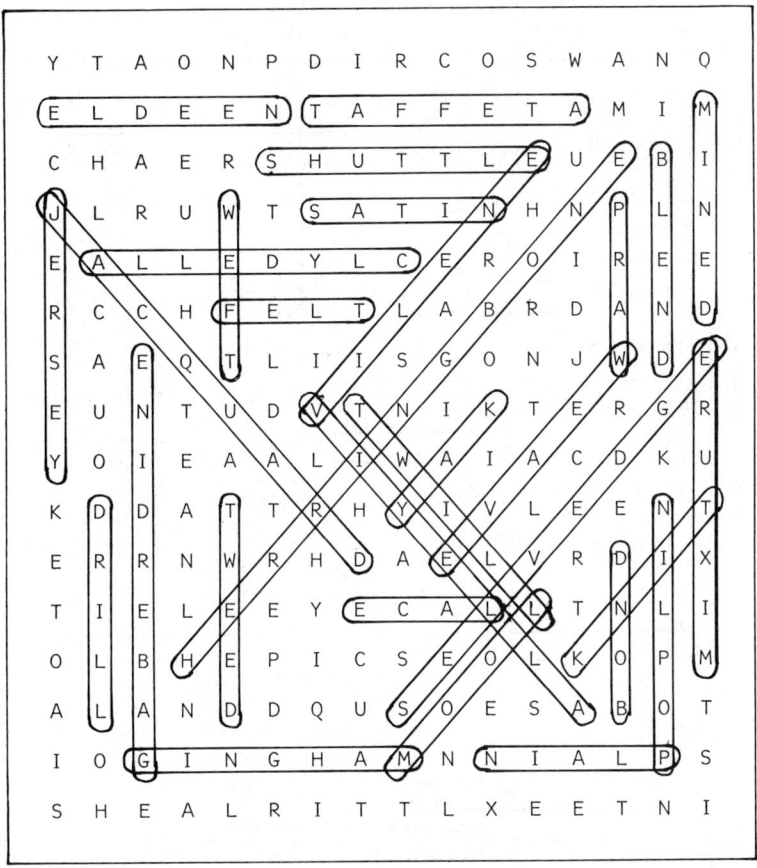

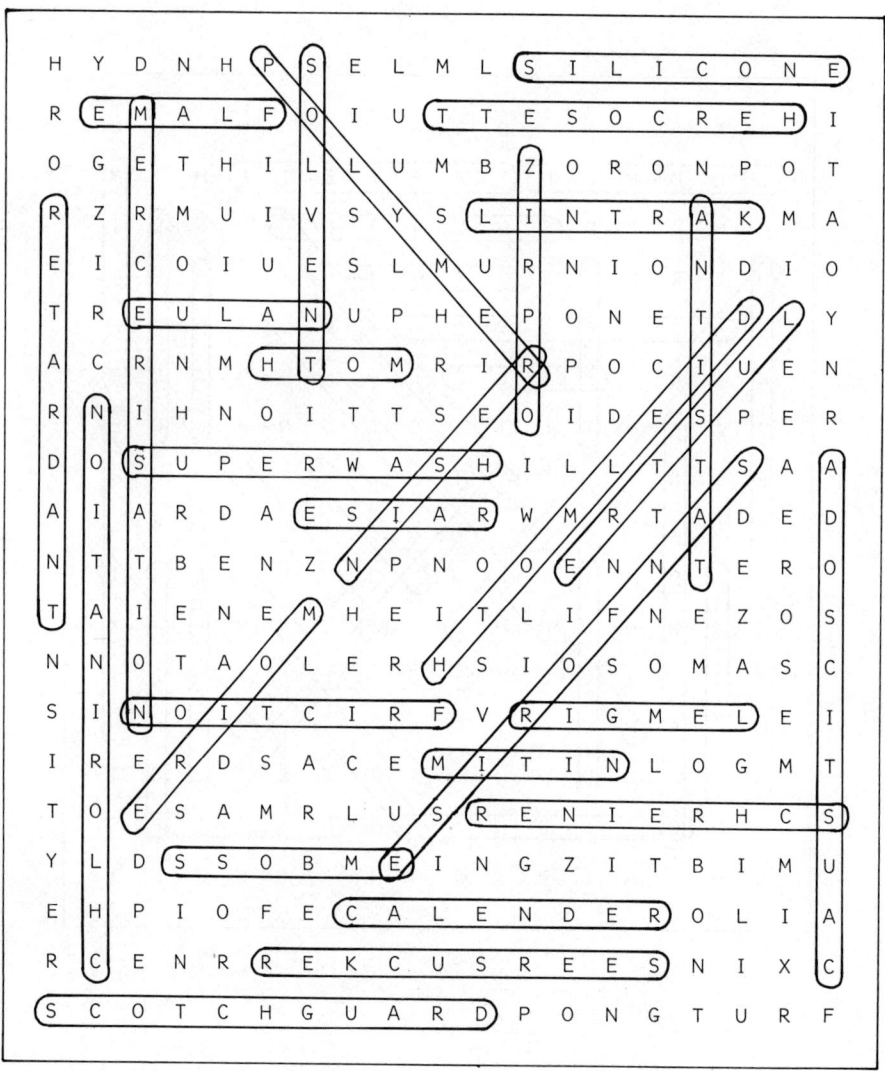

Word search – colour and weaves

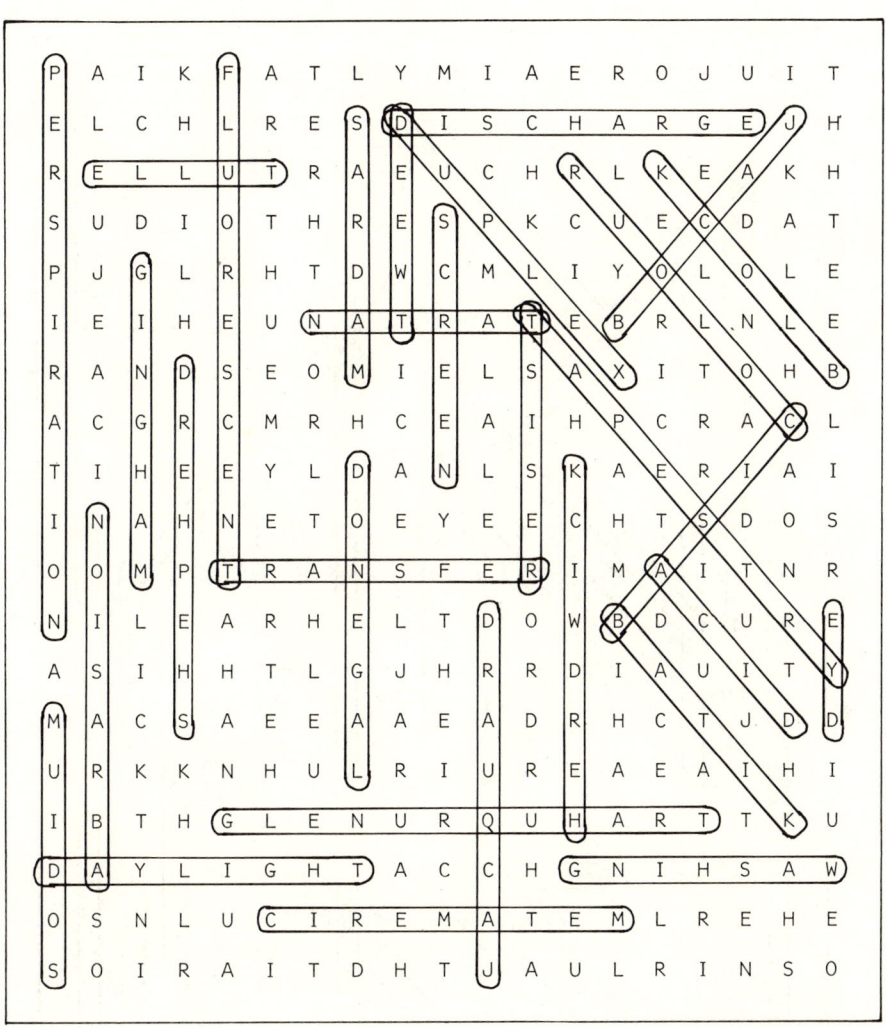

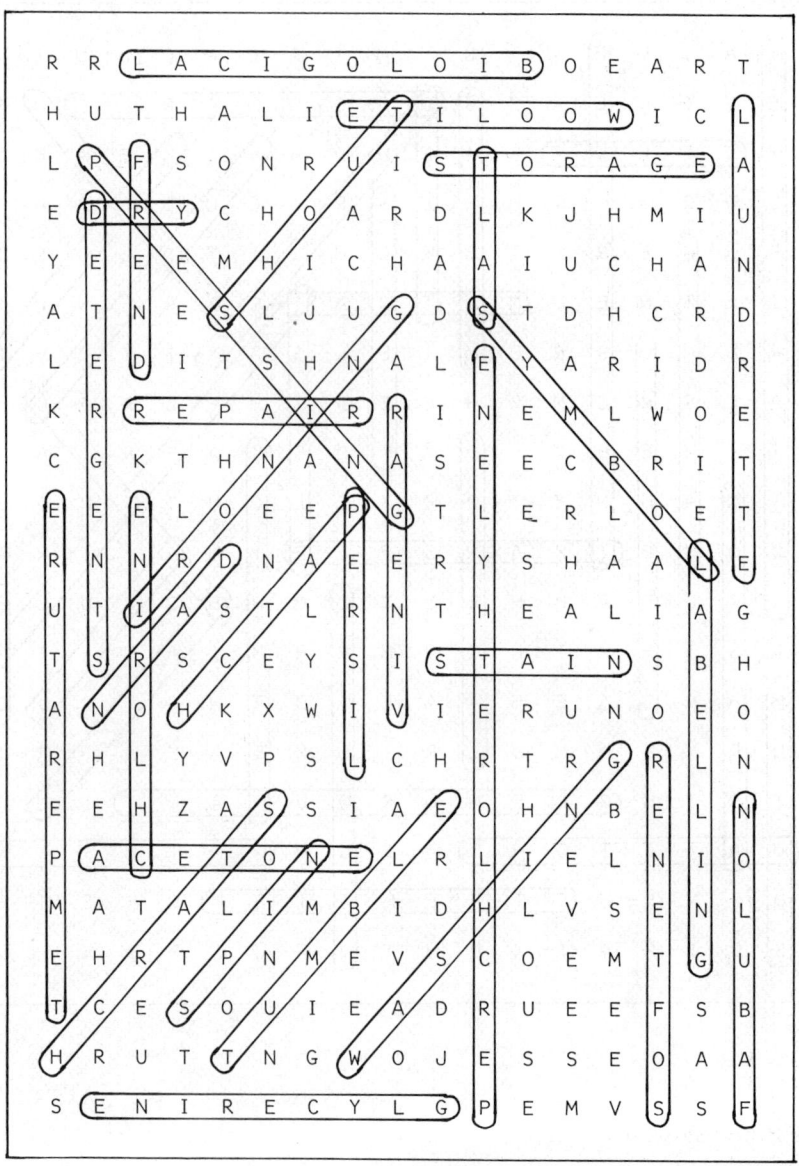

R R L A C I G O L O I B O E A R T
H U T H A L I E T I L O O W I C L
L P F S O N R U I S T O R A G E A
E D R Y C H O A R D L K J H M I U
Y E E M H I C H A A I U C H A N D
A T N E S L J U G D S T D H C R R
L E D I T S H N A L E Y A R I D E
K R R E P A I R R I N E M L W O T
C G K T H N A N A S E E C B R I T
E E L O E E P G T L E R L O E T E
R N N R D N A E E R Y S H A A L G
U T I A S T L R N T H E A L I A H
T R S C E Y S I S T A I N S B E O
A O H K X W I V I E R U N O E O N
R H L Y V P S L C H R T R G R L L
E E H Z A S S I A E O H N B E L I
P A C E T O N E L R L I E L N I O
M A T A L I M B I D H L V S E N L
E H R T P N M E V S C O E M T G U
T C E S O U I E A D R U E E F S B
H R U T T N G W O J E S S E O A A
S E N I R E C Y L G P E M V S S F

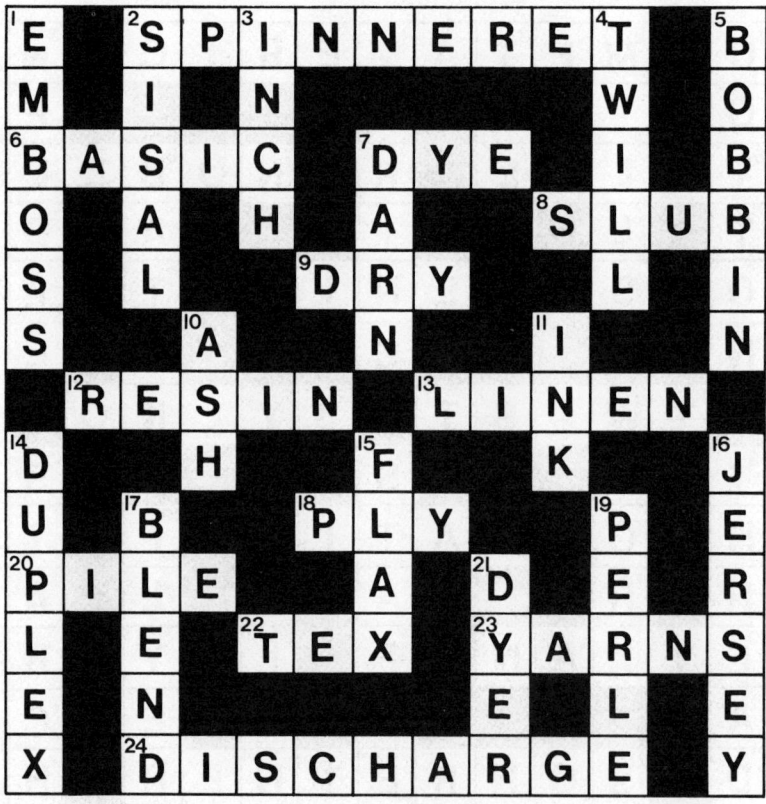